JOURNEY
to ORSAY

M
'O

**Réunion
des Musées
Nationaux**

Edited by Dominique Brisson.

Contributing authors:
Marina Bocquillon-Ferretti,
Valérie Mettais and Laure Murat

Editorial advisors:
Marina Bocquillon-Ferretti,
Anne de Margerie,
Caroline Larroche, Henri Loyrette
and Roland Schaer

Translated by:
Pamela Hargreaves

Designer:
Pierre-Louis Hardy

Cover illustration:
Monet, *La Gare Saint-Lazare*
(*Saint-Lazare Station*), 1877.

Preface

The first visit to a big museum often has much in common with a hiking trip – on which you must, of course, be both sure-footed and suresighted. On such a voyage of discovery and reverie, a compass, map and guide are also needed.

These are what you are offered in this tour around a museum that, paradoxically, was once a departure point for "real" travellers: a station. You will, therefore, be signposted in the right "directions", and to stops at crossroads in history; you will be swept through artistic movements and along paths of exploration, beaconed in the past. Not for a moment will you forget where you are, since the Orsay Museum is itself an "archeological" work from the very era it presents.

One of the original features of this guide is that it answers numerous questions curious minds may ask, as well as supplying information about the exhibits and their historical context. For example: why was such a museographical policy chosen? Why are all the Impressionists up under the roof? Who are the people–both visible and invisible–who work for the museum? Who are the generous donators of so many works on display in the museum today?

The team which produced this "Journey to Orsay" will lead the visitor expertly through the museum and through time, stopping judiciously not only at major works that stand out as landmarks in this prodigious half-century, but also at key personalities. Isn't the best thing about travelling the people you meet?

Françoise CACHIN
Director of the Orsay Museum

Contents

7 **D**estination
Orsay

29 **A**t the crossroads
of the Second Empire
(1848-1870)

57 **T**he Impressionist
Line
(1870-end of the century)

93 **P**assage through
the IIIrd Republic
(1870-1914)

121 **O**n the tracks
of the XXth century
(1900-1914)

ITINERARY
'1

Exploration

■ The origins of a collection
■ Orsay at work
■ Museum statistics

Discoveries

■ The Orsay Museum ballroom
■ Directions for use

Encounter with

■ Victor Laloux, architect

Destination Orsay

by Valérie Mettais

14 July 1900-9 December 1986: more than eighty years elapsed between the inauguration of Orsay Station and the opening of a museum. An adventure which, from Victor Laloux to the ACT architects and Gae Aulenti, leads the visitor through van Gogh's paintings, Rodin's sculptures, Nadar's photographs and Gallé's vases. The station has kept its façade, its size and interior decoration, and now houses the artistic creations of the century that witnessed its construction. There exists a genuine dialogue between two kinds of architecture and two eras. The museum, which is one of the most remarkable in the world, and the first entirely devoted to all the artistic fields of the second half of the XIXth century, exhibits over three thousand works on three levels.

1615

Sale and division of Marguerite de Valois' estate, on the left bank of the Seine, opposite the Louvre.

1700-1708

Charles Boucher d'Orsay, Provost of the Paris merchants, undertook the construction of a quay that was to bear his name.

1810-1838

Jean-Charles Bonnard and Jacques Lacornée built the Palais d'Orsay, assigned to the Cour des Comptes on its completion.

24 May 1871

The Palais d'Orsay destroyed by fire during the Commune.

2 April 1897

The Palais d'Orsay grounds and neighbouring barracks bought by the Chemins de fer d'Orléans to build a station and hotel.

21 April 1898

Architect Victor Laloux's project accepted.

14 July 1900

Inauguration of Orsay Station.

23 November 1939

Closure of mainline service.

March 1973

Station under demolition threat due to plans for a grand hotel.

20 October 1977

The State decided to establish a XIXth century museum in Orsay Station.

5 June 1979

ACT Architecture (Renaud Bardon, Pierre Colboc and Jean-Paul Philippon) won the competition run between six agencies.

16 July 1981

Architect Gae Aulenti was commissioned for the museum's interior design, decoration and furnishings.

1st December 1986

Opening of the Orsay Museum.

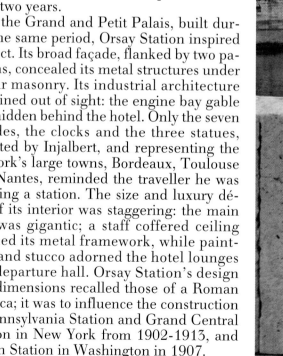

I n 1897, the Compagnie des Chemins de fer d'Orléans looked for a site in the heart of Paris, to build a new passenger station that would serve the South West of France. The ruins of the Cour des Comptes, destroyed by fire during the Commune, stood on a vacant plot of land, very well situated on the left bank, near the Faubourg Saint-Germain and adjacent to the elegant, XVIIIth century Hotel de Salm. The State agreed to relinquish the land: work on the construction of a large, modern station and luxury hotel could begin.

A modern station and a luxury hotel

Victor Laloux was the winner of the competition against the other two architects, Emile Bénard and Lucien Magne. The first trains entered the station at the end of May, 1900, for the opening of the Exposition Universelle. The building was inaugurated on July 14th. It had been completed in less than two years.

Like the Grand and Petit Palais, built during the same period, Orsay Station inspired respect. Its broad façade, flanked by two pavilions, concealed its metal structures under ashlar masonry. Its industrial architecture remained out of sight: the engine bay gable was hidden behind the hotel. Only the seven arcades, the clocks and the three statues, sculpted by Injalbert, and representing the network's large towns, Bordeaux, Toulouse and Nantes, reminded the traveller he was entering a station. The size and luxury décor of its interior was staggering: the main hall was gigantic; a staff coffered ceiling masked its metal framework, while paintings and stucco adorned the hotel lounges and departure hall. Orsay Station's design and dimensions recalled those of a Roman basilica; it was to influence the construction of Pennsylvania Station and Grand Central Station in New York from 1902-1913, and Union Station in Washington in 1907.

But if the eclectic style of its décor related to

PONT ROYAL
CONSTRUIT SOUS LE REGNE DE
LOUIS XIV
1685-1689

the past, its equipment was at the peak of technical progress and worthy of the start of this century: freed from locomotive smoke, it was the first station designed for the electric traction engine. Its fifteen lines handled two hundred trains a day; its inclined planes, elevators, lifts and conveyor belts transported luggage and passengers.

Parisians welcomed their new station with delight and admired its décor and modernity. "The interior of the station on Orsay Quay, whose great architectural splendour and majestic external beauty we are aware of, offers the very latest features which make it one of the most attractive and best-equipped stations in Europe. Everything here works rapidly and automatically; everything is run by electricity", wrote Henry Haguet in *L'Orléans à toute vapeur*.

A five-storey hotel offered the comfort of its three hundred and seventy rooms—most of which had bathrooms—and the luxury of a Louis XVth drawing-room, a reading-room, a ballroom, a dining-room and smoking-room, with their chandeliers, their golden stucco, their woodwork and paintings entrusted to the official artists, Pierre Fritel, Adrien Moreau-Néret, Gabriel Ferrier and Benjamin Constant.

In 1939, Orsay Station closed its mainline service. It was already out of date; its platforms were now too short: the progress in mechanisation that had once been its pride had overtaken it. The building was requisitioned to house prisoners in 1945. It was later used as the filmset for Orson Welles' *The Trial* in 1962, and for some scenes in Bertolucci's *The Conformist* in 1970. It also accommmodated the Renaud-Barrault Theatre and the Drouot auction rooms. With its ornate décor and its uninspired paintings, Orsay Station no longer met with approval; it was just a symbol of turn of the century kitsch, soon to be demolished to make way for a grand hotel.

Then taste changed. The demolition of the Baltard Market in 1973 alerted public opinion and emphasised the urgent need to protect XIXth century architecture. In 1978 it

Victor Laloux

Victor Laloux
(1850-1937).
Orsay Station was
the greatest
achievement of this
French architect,
trained at the Ecole
des Beaux-Arts and
winner of the *grand
Prix de Rome* in
1878. In his official,
academic capacity,
he is also
remembered for his
reconstruction of the
Saint-Martin Basilica
(1886- 1900-1924),
and the building of
the station (1895-
1898) and the
townhall (1896-
1904) in his native
town of Tours.
Outside his
practising career, he
taught architecture
for almost fifty years
at the Ecole des
Beaux-Arts.

The ballroom

The ballroom was situated on the first floor of the Orsay Station Hotel, in the "pavillon aval", above the buffet. From its windows, travellers and guests of the Parisian bourgeoisie's society parties had a magnificent view of the Seine. It was the " favourite setting for wedding receptions, association balls and other heady ceremonies.There is at least one here every day," said Thomas Mann in 1926. With the adjoining Louis Quinze drawing-room and dining-room, the ballroom bears witness to the extreme care taken by the station architect with regard to décor. Victor Laloux effectively designed the hotel interior down to the smallest detail, and chose the artists himself. This ballroom is, thus, a shining example the Neo-Rococo style so popular at the end of the century: the luxurious and ornate décor abounding in fluted columns and pilasters, golden cornices and friezes, cherubim and shell motifs, beribboned mirrors, illuminated garlands and crystal chandeliers. The ceiling is adorned with a Pierre Fritel composition, *Le Char d'Apollon dans une ronde de figures printanières* (*Apollo's Chariot in a Ring of Spring Figures*), and the pendentives and medallions were no doubt executed in his studio.

The ballroom, symbol of the XIXth century's eclectic inspiration, was the natural choice of abode for the paintings and sculptures officially representative of art under the IIIrd Republic. It is the only example in the Orsay Museum where the décor and exhibited works reconstitute the atmosphere of the era.

The origins of a collection

was officially decided to create a museum dedicated to the art and history of the previous century, that would be established in the Orsay Hotel and Station, opposite the Louvre, on the other side of the Seine.

The XIXth century museum: 1848-1914

The Orsay Museum's comprehensive policy embraces all forms of artistic creation in Europe and America: painting, drawing, prints and posters, sculpture, furniture and decorative arts, architecture, photography and the cinema, both of which were born in the XIXth century. The works came from national collections that had been bought by the State for the Luxembourg Museum, dedicated to living XIXth century artists. Before Orsay's opening, they had been exhibited at the Louvre, the Jeu de Paume, in some provincial museums where they were in store, and at the Palais de Tokyo. From 1978 onwards an energetic acquisition policy was undertaken, especially in the fields of architecture, decorative arts, foreign painting and photography.

The period covered spans more than fifty years, from 1848 to 1914, from the beginning of the French IInd Republic to the declaration of the First World War. The Orsay Museum's collections thus lie between those of the Louvre and the National Museum of Modern Art.

1848 was a year of both historical and artistic rupture: insurrections broke out in Europe, leading to political, economic and social upheaval. Arts and techniques were confronted at the first World Fairs, organised in London in 1851 and Paris in 1855. Pre-Raphaelism dawned in England, photography was developed, Realism compelled recognition, and eclecticism asserted itself. At the turn of the XXth century the Orsay Museum exhibits Art Nouveau, the paintings of the Nabis and the late works of Bonnard and Vuillard. However, the chron-

The wealth of the Orsay Museum's national collections springs from several sources.

Purchase
Acquisition of works from private owners, art dealers and auction sales. The museum's purchasing policy, started in 1978, aims at completing its collections and increasing its number of important works. Hence, for example, Gaugin's famous wood relief, *Soyez mystérieuses* (*Be Mysterious*), bought in 1990, and a hundred and fifty photographic portraits by Félix Nadar in 1991.

Dation
Act which, since 1968, permits the donation of works of art in lieu of death-duties: in this way, the Orsay Museum notably acquired numerous paintings by Pierre Bonnard in 1984 and 1988, and Jacques-Emile Blanche's *Portrait of Marcel Proust* in 1989.

Deposition
Works are left in safe keeping by other museums and state bodies. Thus, in 1985, the Museum of Modern Art deposited Henri Matisse's *Luxe, Calme et*

Volupté (*Luxury, Calm and Delight*).

Gift or Donation
Gifts may come from collectors, an artist's descendants, or companies. Certain gifts are subject to special clauses: when held in usufruct, the donator may enjoy the work until his death; one may request that the works be displayed together, as did Moreau-Nélaton, Chauchard and Gachet. The Orsay Museum has received innumerable gifts. To name just a few: Henri Rivière's photographs, Gallé's *La Main aux algues et aux coquillages* (*Hand with Seaweed and Shells*) and, among the most recent, in 1990, a drawing by Degas, *Portrait of Thérèse De Gas Morbilli*, not forgetting, in 1983, the Kodak- Pathé Foundation's entire XIXth century photographic stock, and the Eiffel Fund in 1989.

Bequest
A gift left by will: the museum receives the work on the donator's death. Gustave Caillebotte's legacy of 1894 is the most renowned.

Georges Seurat (1859-1891), *The Black Bow* 1882-1883, conté crayon, 31 × 23 cm. Subtle materialisation of light and shade that emphasises the unknown young woman's elegant silhouette. Seurat's drawings without outlines explore the surface of the paper until they reach a mysterious chiaroscuro.

Literature

Architecture

From children's books to dictionaries, or from Baudelaire to Rimbaud, literature holds a place of honour in one of the dossier-exhibit rooms. Lectures, debates and conferences on the subject are given, and publications are available in the bookshop located in the former station buffet. Over five thousand books on art and history of the second half of the XIXth century, exhibition catalogues and novels are on sale.

**Edouard Manet
(1832-1883),
Reading, 1868,
oil on canvas,
60 × 73 cm.**

In this intimist portrait of his wife and son, Manet's play on harmonies in white and the effects of light, matter and transparency is that of a virtuoso.

The "pavillon amont", from the Opéra Garnier through the dossier-exhibit to the Guimard tower, is dedicated to the museum's collections of architectural fragments, drawings and models, and town decoration and furniture. Orsay Station itself is an extraordinary lesson in architecture.

Photography

History

With more than thirteen thousand works collected since 1979, the Orsay Museum is the first fine art museum in France to regularly present photographs in three temporary exhibition halls. The daguerreotypes, Nadar's portraits and the compositions of the international pictorialist trend illustrate the exceptional creative wealth of this major XIXth century art.

Edward Steichen (1879-1973), *Self-portrait with his wife Clara Smith on their honeymoon at Lake George on Alfred Stieglitz's family estate*, 1903, platinotype, glycerine, 22 × 25 cm.

Steichen, a major figure in American Pictorialism, co-founder with Alfred Stieglitz of the New York group, Photo Secession, experimented with close range compositions, blurred effects and subtle printing techniques.

Films, pictures and exhibits demonstrate the important role played by political, social and economic history in the museum. Immediately on entering, the "Introductory History" recalls the landmarks of the XIXth century through a display of symbolic objects: a flag, a worker's handbook, a typewriter, a general mobilization order, newspapers and posters...

Maximilien Luce (1858-1941), *A Paris Street under the Commune,* 1905, oil on canvas, 151 × 225 cm.

Close to socialist and anarchist circles, and representative, with Seurat and Signac, of Neo- Impressionism, Luce immortalises the massacres of the Commune thirty years later.

Painting

Over one thousand paintings exhibited in the Orsay Museum (with a total collection of more than 2,500) reveal the diverse trends, styles and artists of the last half of the XIXth century: eclectism, Realism, Impressionism, Neo-Impressionism, Naturalism and Symbolism. From the painters then disapproved of to the most official.

Frédéric Bazille (1841-1870), *Bazille's Studio,* 1870, oil on canvas, 98 × 128 cm.

In his vast studio in the rue Condamine, Bazille paints the the portrait of his friends, the future Impressionists: Renoir under the staircase, writer Emile Zola leaning on the bannister, Manet and Monet talking to Bazille and Edmond Maître at the piano.

Sculpture

Sculpture has found an essential place in the Orsay Museum, worthy of the one it held in the XIXth century. The enormity of the station, the immense central aisle and the terraces offer the works space and light, from Carpeaux's fountain to the public monuments of the IIIrd Republic and Rodin's *The Gate of Hell*. Small sculptures and ceramics are found throughout the visit, with official marble statues in the ballroom.

Auguste Rodin (1840-1917), *Jules Dalou,* 1883, bronze, 54 × 45 cm.

With this bust, impressive in its rigourous and powerful relief, Rodin pays hommage to the sculptor of *Triumph of the Republic,* poet of social Naturalism.

Cinema

The Press

The two rooms called "Birth of the Cinema" trace the history of film techniques, from the magic lantern to the Lumière brothers' discoveries in 1895. Excerpts from early films may be seen and an annual festival explores the origins of cinema; short films on art and documentaries on exhibition themes are shown in the auditorium, video library and small rooms throughout the museum.

Shot from the short film *Degas' Little Dancer* by Henri Alekan, choreography by Ethery Pagava, music by Olivier Colé, 6 minutes. Short films produced by the culture department enhance the visitor's appreciation of the museum's collections: from original films to documentaries , they reveal the works in their context.

The "Press Gallery", on the upper level, outlines its history in pictures and texts: from the *Petit Journal,* sold at five centimes, to the articles, society columns, serials and illustrated reviews of the beginning of the century. A frequent exhibition theme.

Jean Béraud (1849-1946), *The Editorial Staff of the Journal des Débats en 1889*, 1889, oil on canvas, 98 × 115 cm.

To celebrate its centenary, the *Journal des Débats* commissioned Béraud, painter-chronicler of the IIIrd Republic, to do a group portrait of its journalists and editorial writers, including Paul Bourget, Taine and Renan.

Music

Decorative Arts

From Schumann to Debussy, XIXth century music is everywhere in the Orsay Museum: in the auditorium during its chamber music recitals, in the restaurant with its recreated atmosphere of the "grands cafés", and in the sound of the piano that accompanies silent film projections. It is also recalled in the Opéra Garnier on the ground floor, in the showcases displaying the gramophone and in the dossier-exhibits.

Edgar Degas (1834-1917), *The Opera Orchestra,* circa 1868-1869, oil on canvas, 56 × 46 cm.

A familiar figure at the Opera, its wings, dressing-rooms, stage, lighting, musicians and dancers had no secrets for Degas who favoured surprising off-centre or ascending view angles and compositions.

The goldsmithery, glassware, ceramics and furniture on show illustrate the prolific production of decorative arts in the XIXth century, and highlight art lovers' tastes and the interior of their homes, offices or dining-rooms.

Edouard Vuillard (1868-1940), *Jeanne Lanvin,* circa 1933, oil on canvas, 124 × 136 cm.

In the 1930s, Vuillard devoted himself to large society portraits that invite one into the privacy of the rich appartments of the upper middle classes.

ological frontiers remain flexible and respect the development of each technique, an artist's career and the evolution of a movement.

It was effectively a question of transforming this station, this departure point, while respecting its originality, its perspective, its framework and décor. Orsay Station became a museum, but was also displayed and put on stage: it was the first "objet d'art" in this XIXth century museum.

The merging of two architectural styles

The execution of such an undertaking was a challenge accepted by the ACT Architecture agency, winner of the State run competition in 1979. The interior design, decoration and furnishings were entrusted to Italian architect and designer Gae Aulenti, who also partially refurbished, in 1985, the rooms of the Pompidou Centre Modern Art Museum.

The initial confrontation between two architectural styles would lead to greater affinity. The station offered its immensity and the towering proportions of its nave, its wide-spanned arches, its metal framework and its glass roof inundated with light. In return, the museum proposed contrasting split volumes, multiplicity of rooms with diversified spaces and the sobre ochre tones of Burgundy stone. Any pastiche of Laloux's eclectic décor was ruled out, to make way for a simple, powerful style playing on contrast. Unity stems from the combination of colour and natural light with artificial lighting. "All forms–partitions, grooved mouldings, screens, inclined planes–were chosen for the lighting, for light control, to see the works of art, and not to illuminate the architecture", stated Gae Aulenti.

The contrast between the two architectural styles remains: everything reminds the visitor that he is still walking through a station:

the staff coffers and glass roof of the nave's vaulted ceiling, the marquise, the clocks, the steel structures and the stucco decoration waiting to be discovered.

Once railway tracks stretched down the museum's long, central aisle, which rises, level by level, to two towers built in front of the glazed tympanum that closes the general perspective. On the ground floor, an extensive number of rooms have been created on either side of this wide, median hall. Overlooking terraces make up the middle level; the two galleries on the upper level, under the glass roof, benefit from the natural lighting.

Every part of the station has been used, but the circulation flow has been reconsidered. Visitors' access to the museum is from the rue de Bellechasse under the marquise. The former travellers' exit is now the public reception area. The buffet has been transformed into a bookshop, with two entrances from the quay and the interior. A café is located in the pavilion known as the "pavillon aval." The hotel ballroom, "la salle des fêtes," with its restored rococo décor, exhibits paintings and sculptures of the IIIrd Republic. Lastly, the dining-room once more fulfils its original vocation in becoming the museum restaurant.

A walk on three levels

The presentation on three levels enables the

View of the nave. The immensity of the 32-metre-high nave immediately strikes the visitor on entering. There are then around 3,000 exhibits waiting to be discovered.

museum to exhibit a wide variety of works and to reveal all parts of the former station. Techniques, styles and artists are displayed separately. As a general rule, there is no mixing of genres, nor atmosphere or interior reconstitution. Mirroring the taste and choice of great art lovers, certain rooms group collections together in respect of the donator's wishes, as in the case of Etienne Moreau-Nélaton in 1906, Alfred Chauchard in 1909, Paul Gachet from 1949-1954, or Max and Rosy Kaganovitch in 1973.

The works are exhibited in chronological order: the ground floor is devoted to art under the Second Empire, and the pavilion known as the "pavillon amont" reveals its steel structures and covers architecture and some furniture; the visit continues on the upper level, where the natural light through the glass roof makes the "galerie des Hauteurs" the most fitting place to introduce Impressionism and Post-Impressionism; finally, the domed rooms of the middle level display the works of the IIIrd Rebublic. As the visitor moves up and then down, he is constantly surprised by his encounters with architecture, the works and their unique exhibit space. The latter lends itself to the varied nature of the works shown: vast rooms and open terraces for the large canvases and sculptures, smaller, softly-lit rooms for the drawings and photographs.

In designated areas parallel to the main tour, one may discover the context of the works in history, literature and music: the Press Gallery, "passage de la presse," the Introduction to History, "ouverture sur l'histoire," the Birth of the Cinema, "naissance du cinématographe," a large temporary exhibition space, several "dossier exhibit" rooms and an auditorium.

When the Orsay Museum opened its doors to the public, on the 9th December, 1986, every visitor was free to follow his own itinerary between each level, on the terraces, through the reception rooms and halls. Thanks to its renovation and exhibition policies, Orsay is a place which favours all discoveries.

Directions for use

Suggested route

The museum visit stretches over three levels. The first part, on the ground floor, covers the painting, sculpture, decorative arts and architecture of the Second Empire period.
The second part, on the upper level, continues with Impressionist and Post-Impressionist painting.
The last part, on the middle level, diplays the decorative arts of the IIIrd Republic, sculptures and public monuments, official paintings, the Symbolists, foreign schools, architecture and decorative arts of Art Nouveau and the Vienna, Glasgow and Chicago schools, and, finally, post 1900 painting.

Temporary exhibitions and special events

On the ground floor is a vast, independant exhibition area used for the Orsay Museum's major exhibitions, such as those on Chicago, Cézanne, van Gogh in Paris, Munch and France, Guimard, etc. The trimestrial, multidisciplinary dossier-exhibits are held in seven rooms throughout the museum. Numerous museum events take place in the auditorium on the ground floor: lectures, debates and courses, concerts and films. Musical presentations are also given in the ballroom and restaurant on Thursday evenings and Sunday afternoons; films are shown in the video library and small rooms.

Documentary resources

Throughout the visit, "key points", or presentation cards, can be found. In the consultation room above the Rooftop Café, a picture databank, video library and exhibition catalogues provide extensive information on the museum's collections.

Guided tours

Guided tours on a specific work, artist or artistic trend are available as well as the complete museum tour.

Educational facilities

An area of 600 square metres is reserved for young visitors from the age of 5 to 15: it includes a reference room, workshop, and computer and audiovisual studios. Several different visits are at their disposal.

Practical information

Main entrance: 1, rue de Bellechasse.
Temporary exhibition entrance: place Henri de Montherlant.
Postal address: 62, rue de Lille, 75343 Paris cedex 07.
Telephone: 45 49 48 14
General information recording: 45 49 11 11
The museum is open from 10 am to 6 pm on Tuesday, Wednesday, Friday and Saturday, from 9 am to 6 pm on Sunday, from 10 am to 9.45 pm on Thursday. Closed on Monday. "Carte Blanche" membership offers free access to the museum and exhibitions.
The Reception area includes a bookshop, cardshop, boutique (outside access), exchange bureau, telephones, postbox, first-aid post, audioguide rental and guide sales counter.
A restaurant is located on the middle level and a café on the upper level.

ground floor
first part of the visit

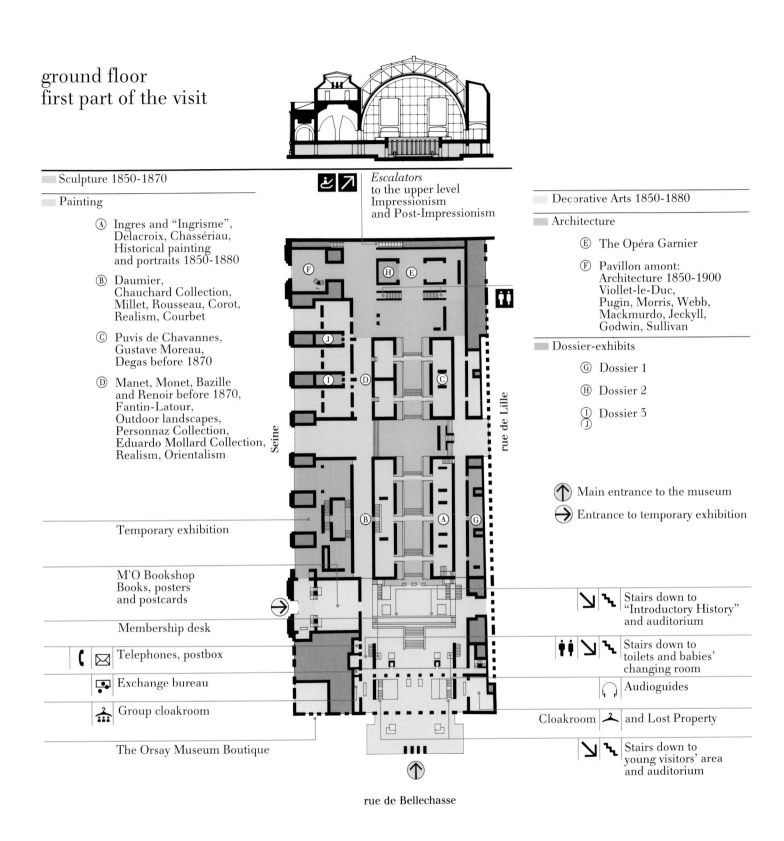

■ Sculpture 1850-1870

▨ Painting

Ⓐ Ingres and "Ingrisme",
Delacroix, Chassériau,
Historical painting
and portraits 1850-1880

Ⓑ Daumier,
Chauchard Collection,
Millet, Rousseau, Corot,
Realism, Courbet

Ⓒ Puvis de Chavannes,
Gustave Moreau,
Degas before 1870

Ⓓ Manet, Monet, Bazille
and Renoir before 1870,
Fantin-Latour,
Outdoor landscapes,
Personnaz Collection,
Eduardo Mollard Collection,
Realism, Orientalism

Escalators
to the upper level
Impressionism
and Post-Impressionism

■ Decorative Arts 1850-1880

■ Architecture

Ⓔ The Opéra Garnier

Ⓕ Pavillon amont:
Architecture 1850-1900
Viollet-le-Duc,
Pugin, Morris, Webb,
Mackmurdo, Jeckyll,
Godwin, Sullivan

■ Dossier-exhibits

Ⓖ Dossier 1

Ⓗ Dossier 2

Ⓘ Dossier 3
Ⓙ

⬆ Main entrance to the museum

➡ Entrance to temporary exhibition

Seine

rue de Lille

Temporary exhibition

M'O Bookshop
Books, posters
and postcards

Membership desk

☏ ✉ Telephones, postbox

Exchange bureau

Group cloakroom

The Orsay Museum Boutique

Stairs down to
"Introductory History"
and auditorium

Stairs down to
toilets and babies'
changing room

🎧 Audioguides

Cloakroom and Lost Property

Stairs down to
young visitors' area
and auditorium

rue de Bellechasse

upper level
second part of the visit

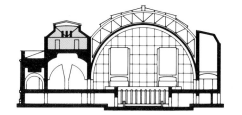

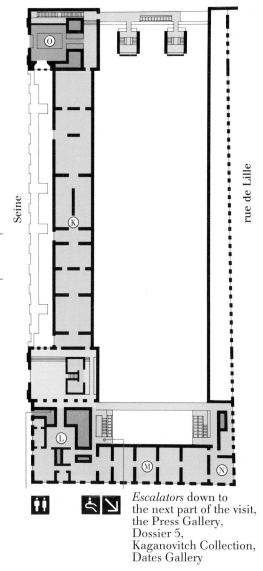

■ Painting

   Ⓚ Impressionism:
      Moreau-Nélaton Collection,
      Whistler, Manet, Degas,
      Monet, Renoir, Pissaro,
      Sisley, Cézanne

      Degas (pastels)

   Ⓛ Van Gogh,
      Gachet Collection

      Redon,
      pastels

   Ⓜ Douanier-Rousseau,
      Pont-Aven School:
      Gauguin, Bernard, Sérusier

      Neo-Impressionism:
      Seurat, Signac, Cross, Luce

   Ⓝ Toulouse-Lautrec,
      small paintings

■ Dossier-exhibits

   Ⓞ Dossier 4 (on 3 levels)

■ Rooftop Café

      Consultation room
      above the Rooftop Café:
      video and audiotape library,
      picture database,
      catalogues

Escalators down to
the next part of the visit,
the Press Gallery,
Dossier 5,
Kaganovitch Collection,
Dates Gallery

middle level
last part of the visit

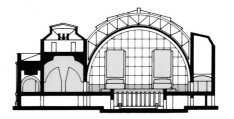

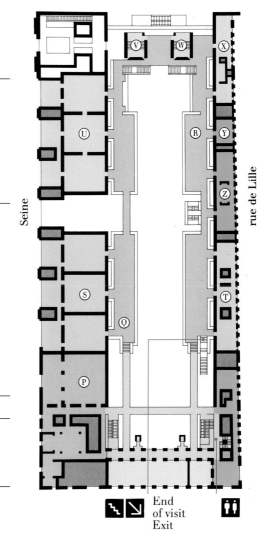

⬛ Sculpture

   Ⓟ Decorative Arts
of the Third Republic

   Ⓠ Barrias, Coutan,
Fremier, Gérôme, Rodin

   Ⓡ Desbois, Rosso,
Bartholomé, Bourdelle,
Maillol, Joseph Bernard

⬛ Painting

   Ⓢ Painting from the
1880-1900 Salon,
Naturalism,
Foreign schools,
Symbolism

   Ⓣ Bonnard, Denis, Vallotton,
Vuillard, Roussel

⬛ Art Nouveau

   Ⓤ France, Belgium,
Guimard,
Ecole de Nancy,
Gallé,
Carabin, Charpentier,
Dampt

   Ⓥ Guimard

   Ⓦ International
Art Nouveau

   Ⓧ Vienna, Glasgow,
Chicago

⬛ Birth of the Cinema

⬛ Dossier-exhibits

   Ⓨ Dossier 6

   Ⓩ Dossier 7

⬛ Restaurant

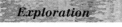

Orsay at work

Museum statistics

Who works at the Orsay Museum? Over 700 people including about 550 permanent staff:
- a scientific team made up of curators and documentalists, who are involved in enriching the collections and the care and presentation of works, who prepare exhibitions and catalogues and compile information on the artists and pieces;
- a cultural team of around twenty people, in charge of organising educational activities, producing films, creating concert, lecture and cinema programmes and developing services offered to museum members;
- a team of museum personnel to welcome visitors, to ensure their security and that of their belongings, to issue tickets and to sell books and reproductions;
- numerous other departments figure in museum life: communication, technical, financial and administrative services coexist with workshops: photographers, fitters, restorers, draughtsmen, printers, etc. all of whom are necessary in this complex company that the museum also is.

The station

380 workmen undertook the construction of the station from 1898 to 1900
Length of interior: 220 m
Width of interior: 75 m
Hall: length: 138 m, width: 40 m, height: 32 m
Weight of metallic framework: 12,000 tons
Floor area: 30,000 m²
Structural area: 110,000 m²
Glazed area: 35,000 m²
Total track length: 3,650 m
Traffic: 200 trains a day

The museum

1,200 workers undertook the construction of the museum from 1983 to 1986
Floor area: 47,000 m²
Covered ground and wall area: 30,000 m²
Public reception area: 2,450 m²
Permanent exhibition space: 16,000 m²
Temporary exhibition space: 1,200 m²
Auditorium: 347 seats, 570 m²
10 escalators, 6 lifts and elevators Approximately 700 people work in the museum
The museum can welcome 5,500 visitors at a time
2.8 million visitors in 1991, an average of 9,000 people a day
16 million visitors since 1986

The collections

Approximately 3,000 works exhibited
Approximately 6,000 works preserved:
2,620 paintings, 1,040 on display
1,260 sculptures, 670 on display
1,520 objets d'art, 800 on display
250 pastels, 90 on display
360 documentary pieces, 310 on display
Approximately 13,000 photographs

Victor Laloux, architect

The inauguration of Orsay Station on the 14th July, 1900, was the crowning success in the career of a fifty-year-old architect: Victor Alexandre Frédéric Laloux. Born in Tours, he served an academic apprenticeship that led to official commissions for public buildings. He graduated from the Ecole des Beaux-Arts in 1877, and, a year later, won the Grand Prix de Rome, the subject of which was to design a cathedral. Respectful of his masters' teachings, Laloux drew his inspiration from the past and referred to St. Peter's of Rome. "He likes imposing, sumptuous, lofty works; a temperament [...]. No inventiveness, no search for originality, but a remarkable understanding of size and grandeur," noted the jury.

Laloux's first executed work, to which he always remained attached, was the reconstruction of the Saint-Martin de Tours Basilica, begun in 1886-1890 and completed in 1898-1902. The saint's image would later be found on one of the cartouches decorating Orsay Station. The Basilica's simplicity, golden domes and mosaic decorations are reminiscent of Roman, Byzantine and medieval art. This was Laloux's first architectural work in an eclectic style: born out of skilfully-blended past references.

Laloux then turned his hand to railway stations, once more in his hometown. From 1896-1898 he applied a stone façade–worthy of a Greek temple–and cast iron ornamentation to the metallic structures of Tours Station. No sign must be left of the iron, which cannot, said Laloux, "furnish by itself, with its joints, surfaces and industrial workmanship, truly estimable

The station façade in Tours, 1895-1898. Laloux erected a stone façade at the end of the station. Semi-circular pylons, adorned with sculptures, and crowned with figures representing the network's large towns, separate the glazed bays.

decorative expression." Orsay Station and Hotel still bear witness to this. Built in an upper-class district, the new passenger station concealed its metal skeleton. Laloux won the competition on this profession of faith: "Only stone must be visible in the future station, only stone could replace the Cour des Comptes and face the Tuileries."

In liason with the railway company's engineers, Laloux set to work. Since there was no longer any smoke, thanks to electrification, the architect planned high-ceilinged rooms. A surbased arch, adorned with staff coffers, masked the metal framework. Inspired by the architecture of Roman baths and basilicas, Laloux was the first to apply their principles to the field of railway buildings. Outside, the hotel façade was erected in front of the station's metal gable.

Laloux gratified the whims of his era. Thus, with its traditional façade, he integrated the station into the town, hid its functional nature, and left the passer-by only an occasional clue: a clock, statues symbolic of towns or Mercury, the god of travellers. "The station is superb and looks like a Fine Arts Academy, and as the Palais des Beaux-Arts resembles a station, I suggest that Laloux should make an exchange, if there is still time," proposed the painter Edouard Detaille.

Laloux was also the architect of Tours and Roubaix's townhalls, which, built in 1897-1904 and 1907-1911, were once more marked by their simplicity of design and ornate decoration. He completed his last major work, the Crédit Lyonnais' head offices in Paris, in 1907-1913.

Head inset:
Adolphe Dechenaud (1868-1926),
Victor Laloux, 1912 (?)
oil on canvas, 55 × 47 cm

ITINERARY
'2

Exploration

- Haussmann's Paris
- Daumier and his incisive genius
- Furniture: eclecticism under Napoleon III
- Sculptural mediums
- The dawning of Impressionism

Discoveries

- Couture's *The Romans in the Period of Decadence*
- Courbet's *Burial at Ornans*
- The architecture of the Palais Garnier Opera
- Manet's *Olympia*
- Nadar's *Portrait of Baudelaire*
- Carpeaux's *The Dance*

Encounter with

- Baudelaire and Zola, writers and critics

At the crossroads of the Second Empire (1848-1870)

by Laure Murat

The years 1848-1870 might seem like a period of artistic confusion. Between a revolution and a war, styles were reinterpreted and interwoven as the Neoclassical, Neo-Gothic and Neo-Renaissance movements developed. Eclecticism reigned. But this century of progress and change, torn by religious, economic and political strife, also saw the birth of the modern era with Realism and Manet's first paintings.

1848

The February Revolution: end of the July monarchy, fall of Louis-Philippe and proclamation of the IInd Republic.

1849

Courbet's *Burial at Ornans* greeted with scandal.

1851

2 December: Louis-Napoleon Bonaparte's coup d'état. He became Emperor of the French.

1853

Haussmann appointed Prefect of the Seine. Construction of the Palais de l'Industrie by Hittorff in Paris.

1855

Opening of the Paris Exposition Universelle: over 5 million visitors. Courbet, refused admission at the Exposition, launched his "Realism's independant pavilion" where he presented *The Painter's Studio. True Allegory.*

1857

Publication of *Manifeste du réalisme* by novelist and art critic Jules Champfleury.

1859

France declared war against Austria. Japanese art discovered. Photographs included in the Salon for the first time.

1861

Charles Garnier began work on the Opéra de Paris, completed in 1875.

1863

Opening of the "Salon des Refusés". Public scandal caused by Manet's *Le Déjeuner sur l'herbe.* Death of Eugène Delacroix.

1865

Further scandal at the Salon with Manet's *Olympia*, painted in 1863.

1866

First colour photographs.

1867

Opening of the Paris Exposition Universelle: 11 million visitors. Death of Ingres and Baudelaire.

1869

Inauguration of the Suez Canal. Uproar caused by Carpeaux's *The Dance* at the unveiling of the Palais Garnier façade.

1870

19 July: France declared war against Prussia. 2 September: defeated at Sedan. 4 September: proclamation of the IIIrd Republic.

The different artistic trends in the Second Empire deserve more than just an amused or complacent passing glance. Born under Louis-Philippe, after the Romantic period and before Impressionism, they exerted their influence until the end of the XIXth century and crystallised all the tension known in "the most retrospective of centuries" (Saint-Beuve), era of progress but also of immobilism, which saw the evolution of a society dominated by a triumphant bourgeoisie that looked towards history to create its décor.

The 1848 Revolution, which marked the end of the July monarchy and the beginning of the short-lived IInd Republic, did not impede the rise of the new dominant class. Louis-Napoleon Bonaparte became Emperor of the French following the coup d'état of December 2nd, 1851.

Art at the Salon: pastiche and hybrid

The bourgeosie of the Second Empire made up the growing number of spectators at the Salons, organised by the imperial government, under the firm hand of the Count of Nieuwerkerke, Director of Museums and later head of the Beaux-Arts. The two masters of the day were Eugène Delacroix, high priest of colour and leader of Romanticism, never without official commissions, and Jean Auguste Dominique Ingres , whose genius as a draughtsman inspired his pupils (Amaury-Duval, Hyppolite Flandrin, the "neo-Greek" Gérôme) and his followers (Alexandre Cabanel, William Bouguereau). A retrospective of their works at the 1855 Exposition Universelle paid respect to these two authorities who generally dominated the beginning of the Second Empire, as certain major late works attest: Ingres' *La Vierge à l'hostie* (*The Virgin and the Host*) 1855, and *La Source* (*The Spring*) 1856, or Delacroix's *La Chasse aux Lions* (*The Lion Hunt*) 1854.

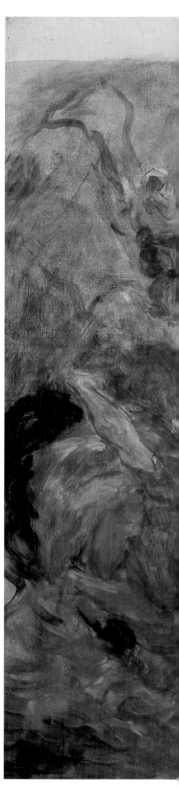

Eugène Delacroix
(1798-1863)
The Lion Hunt, 1854,
oil sketch,
86 × 115 cm.

This sketch for a
canvas exhibited at
the 1855 Salon,
depicts the ferocity
of wild animals and
expresses the
dramatic power of
colour, a lesson
Fauvism would
retain...

Thomas Couture

Les Romains de la décadence
(The Romans in the Period of Decadence)
1847
oil on canvas, 466 × 775 cm

Thomas Couture
(1815-1879).
Couture entered
Gros' studio in 1830,
then became Paul
Delaroche's pupil. In
1837, he won the
second Prix de Rome
and, in 1844, had his
first success at the
Salon with *L'Amour
de l'or. (Love of
Gold). Les Romains
de la décadence (The
Romans in the
Period of Decadence)*
consecrated his
career in 1847. As a
result, he
established himself
as leader of the new
French school. He
had numerous
students, the most
famous being Manet.
He left unfinished
his large, official
commissions, *Les
Enrôlements des
volontaires de 1792
(Enlistment of the
1792 Volunteers)* and
*Le Baptême du
Prince impérial (The
Imperial Prince's
Baptism)*.

Thomas Couture was greeted as
"Thomas Veronese" at the 1847
Salon when he presented his vast
composition, *Les Romains de la
décadence*, its architectural setting
reminiscent of the Italian master's
The Marriage at Cana. The
painting won the gold medal in the
top category and was the crowning
point of Couture's career.
The subject of the *Romans*,
borrowed from Trimalcion's feast
as described by Petronius in his
Satyricon, was, in the Salon
catalogue, accompanied by these
lines from Juvenal's sixth *Satire*,
"Vice, a scourge more cruel than
war, has swooped down on Rome to
avenge the vanquished universe."
The work called attention to noble,
historical painting drawn from
Antiquity, whose inspiration
Couture wished to recapture. He
denounced the widespread problem
of worldly decadence, a direct
allusion to society under Louis-
Philippe. However, to avoid the
bourgeoisie classing the painting as
a vulgar mirror of the era, Couture
took care to set the lascivious and
sprawling figures in opposition to
the hieratical attitudes of the
statues placed between the
columns, embodiments of law and
order to ensure the work's moral
significance. The abased bodies,
prostrate in their wantonness, make
one last attempt to rise or let
themselves slip into a fatal sleep:
the philosophers' reproachful
glance and the promise of
chastisement hover over the dying
members of the party. To depict
this pagan tragedy, Couture drew
his inspiration from not only
Veronese, but from XVIIth century
French painting, from Raphaël and
also Rubens whose influence was
pointed out by the critic Thoré, for
whom the dancer with naked
breasts on the left recalled Envy in
The Queen's Government, now at

the Louvre.
Praised by Théophile Gautier,
eulogised by Fromentin ("There is
only one outstanding work at the
Salon: it's a *Roman Orgy* by a young
man who has brilliantly confirmed

his reputation this year," he wrote to his mother), the canvas was even accepted by Delacroix who was doubtless reminded of *La Mort de Sardanapale* (*The Death of Sardanapale*): "Couture's painting pleased me," he confessed in his diary. As the successor of David, Gros and Géricault in the great French tradition, Couture reached his zenith with *The Romans*. The large compositions later undertaken which may have rivalled this loud "piece of painting" remained unfinished, while the artist's image faded.

Apart from the production of these two masters, whose influence gradually declined, artists tried to find a balance by mixing genres and trends. For example, Théodore Chassériau's *Tépidarium; salle où les femmes de Pompeï venaient se reposer et se sécher en sortant du bain* (*Tepidarium; Room where the Women of Pompeii came to Rest and to Dry themselves after Bathing*) 1853, illustrates the influence of Thomas Couture's *Romains de la décadence* (*The Romans in the Period of Decadence*) the great success of the 1847 Salon, and, at the same time, is Neoclassical in its subject, Romantic and Orientalist in its colours and treatment. Springing from Romanticism and Orientalism, a nascent Symbolism materialised with Gustave Moreau, whose "poet-goldsmith's watercolours", as praised by the Goncourt brothers, "seemed washed with the glow, the patina, of the treasures from *A Thousand and One Nights*". At this time, however, other writer-crictics like Théophile Gautier, Charles Baudelaire and Emile Zola complained about the poverty of exhibitions where narrow, official art prevailed. The severity of the jury, composed exclusively of Beaux-Arts Academy members from 1857 onwards, gave rise to numerous recriminations: the Institute had become a compulsory step for artists along the road to recognition and desirous of commissions to decorate great public buildings; from 1861, Puvis de Chavannes specialised in this genre, executing vast compositions inspired by the Italian Primitives. Although receptive to Ingres' Classicism, he nevertheless opened the way to Symbolism with his allegories bathed in still, peaceful light, and later influenced Georges Seurat, followed by the Nabis.

The Salon public's taste then turned to flattering, narrative historical painting (battle scenes, already appreciated under the Ist Empire, enjoyed a huge success with works by Meissonier, Yvon, Bellangé, John Lewis-Brown), and accomplished and discreetly executed mythological subjects that brought Antiquity to life. At the same time, the irre-

Alexandre Cabanel (1823-1889), *The Birth of Venus*, 1863, oil on canvas, 130 × 225 cm.

Stereotype of official taste under the Second Empire, painted in 1863, the same year as Manet's *Olympia* and *Le Déjeuner sur l'herbe*, it was a huge success at the Salon and charmed Napoleon III who bought it for his personal collection.

Jean-Léon Gérôme (1824-1904), *Young Greeks Holding a Cock Fight*, 1846, oil on canvas, 143 × 204 cm.

This Neo-Greek painting illustrates the taste for smooth treatment and resplendent marmoreal bodies.

Rosa Bonheur (1822-1899), *Ploughing in the Nivernais Region*, 1849, oil on canvas, 134 × 260 cm.

Animal labour in country life: a favourite theme of this artist who was head of the Imperial Drawing School for young people.

Alexandre Antigna (1817-1878), *Corpus Christi*, 1855, oil on canvas, 140 × 195 cm.

Antigna witnessed the religious revival in XIXth century France: childhood is here a metaphor of society.

Franz-Xaver Winterhalter (1806-1873), *Portrait of Madame Rimsky-Korsakov,* 1864, oil on canvas, 117 × 90 cm.

She sat with her hair loose and her bodice unfastened: the painting's boldness springs more from its model than from its highly conventional treatment.

Haussmann's Paris

pressible rise in popularity of the portrait by artists like Franz-Xaver Winterhalter and Dubuffe coincided with the evolution of photography. Landscape painting, championed by Decamps, found, parallel to official circuits, new resources in Corot and the Barbizon school who were to influence the future Impressionists, Sisley, Renoir and Monet...

Eclecticism in all the arts

The diversity of trends and their combination, which, for the sake of convenience, we call "eclecticism", was to be found in all the arts.

First, architecture, whose variety of styles was apparent in all the great building projects of the Second Empire, at the time Baron Haussmann was organising Paris' transfiguration: the linking of the Louvre with the Tuileries under Lefuel and Visconti, Duc's transformation of the Palais de Justice, Labrouste's Bibliothèque Nationale, Duban's Ecole des Beaux-Arts and the development of Neo-Renaissance, Viollet-le-Duc's Neo-Gothic "restoration" of the Château de Pierrefonds, and, finally, Constant-Dufeux's illustration of the Neo-Greek trend in his official buildings' projects. The "great works" had one thing in common: the architects constructed over old, already existing elements which they used to create a strong, recognisable, coherent effect. Their compositions were more like genuine creations yielding to the demands of "archeology". These reinterpretations also gave birth to buildings in their own right, like the Cathedral of Marseilles, erected by Vaudoyer who employed all the resources of religious vocabulary. The new Opera, designed by Charles Garnier, considered as the monument epitomising most of the artistic preoccupations of the Second Empire, at times conceals the importance of these other contemporary works that reveal their architects' flexibility.

From 1853-1869, under the guiding hand of Baron Haussmann, Prefect of the Seine, the old Paris was transformed into a light, recognisable and organised town. This project involved the total restructuring of Paris: the great centres were cleared and then linked by "straight and symmetrical" avenues modelled on Le Nôtre's principles; the boulevard Saint-Germain, day: restoration of the Palais de Justice, erection of the Tribunal de Commerce, Lefuel and Visconti's refurbishing of the Louvre. For political and economic reasons, Haussmann, working in strict collaboration with the Emperor, who had been deeply impressed by London's organisation, thus "cleansed" the city of its seats of potential insurrection, and ensured the prosper-

The construction of the Opéra du Palais Garnier led to changes in the whole area and the building of radial avenues in conformity with classical style. The model of the Opera and its district is found at the back of the museum nave.

the rue de Rivoli, the avenue de l'Opéra and the boulevard de Sébastopol were all built at this time. The project also included a sanitation (sewers, road renovation and paving, gas street-lighting) and construction programme; in a climate of feverish speculation, buildings and monuments worthy of the capital city of an Empire saw the ity of modern Paris. If the new town, divided into twenty arrondissements in 1859, and linked to the outside by its stations, incurred battered Parisians' recriminations, it nonetheless became the future model for a considerable number of world capitals.

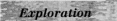

Sculptural mediums

Jean-Baptiste known as **Auguste Clésinger** (1814-1883),
Woman Bitten by a Snake, 1847, marble, 56.5 × 180 cm.
The artist's first success, this nude's eroticism created
a scandal. Due to his frequent and sensuous use of marble,
Clésinger was often compared to Michelangelo and Puget.

Sculpture, during the Second Empire, was one of the disciplines that underwent the greatest number of technical changes. One of the new techniques enabled the mass-production of reduced scale bronzes. This "multiple" phenomena led to a boom in trade and changed the status of the sculptor, henceforth under contract to a smelter-publisher, as in the Pradier-Susse or Rude-Barbedienne associations. Furthermore, pliant materials (clay, plaster, wax), which were more easily mastered and more often used than working directly on marble, gave scope to new methods and effects. If the smooth sculptures of the XVIIIth century left no trace of the sculptor's tools, those of the XIXth century, on the contrary, enabled one to follow the evolution of a work. Carpeaux was,

for example, the first to let the lumps and coils of the clay he was moulding be seen. Barye, Mène and Degas took a renewed interest in wax and resin: their plasticity allowed the artist to change a movement, modify a gesture or hold a pose. This mixing of mediums was accompanied by the introduction and use of natural or artificial polychromy. The constant supply of onyx from the Algerian quarries, discovered during the country's colonisation, the prevailing Orientalist craze, and the revelation of colour on ancient monuments encouraged sculptors like Cordier to adopt a bolder approach.

From work of art to ornament, from monument to document, XIXth century sculpture threw its methods into upheaval and diversified its functions.

Jean-Louis-Ernest Meissonier (1815-1891),
The Traveller, 1878, red wax, fabric, metal
and leather, 47.8 × 60 × 39.5 cm.
For the statuette and its base, the artist used two separate
beeswax mixes and thus shows the mediums'
different renderings.

Jean-Baptiste Carpeaux (1827-1875), *The Imperial Prince and his Dog Nero*, 1865, plaster, 43.8 × 16.1 cm.

Commissioned by the Empress, this statue representing her son, and very different from Carpeaux's early Romantic works, was executed at the same time as his decoration of the south façade on the Pavillon de Flore at the Louvre.

Charles Garnier

The Opéra Garnier
1860-1875

Charles Garnier (1825-1898). Appointed architect of the Opéra de Paris (1861-1875), he devoted himself almost exclusively to this construction, in which he established the basic model for theatres to come. He would also build the Cercle de la Librairie (1880) and the Panorama français (1882) in Paris, the Observatory in Nice, and the Casino and thermal resort in Vittel (1882).

The Opéra de Paris alone represents a page in French architectural history. The monument that is today considered as a reference to Napoleon IIIrd style and a symbol of Haussmann's Paris was the work of one man: Charles Garnier, who undertook its construction in 1860 and finished it in 1875. Between these two dates, the architect, whose project had been unanimously accepted by the official competition jury, himself assumed all responsibility for its execution, from the building site to the decorative and iconographic programme, whether sculpted or painted. All this, in spite of political disorder. Society's temple of pleasure under the Second Empire, situated in a fast-expanding business area, the Opera, when the regime fell, became the symbol of the now-hated former government's excessive expenditure. The Palais Garnier's image suffered in more than one respect from this change in politics: although the monument's completion was helped by the fire at the opera house in the rue Le Peletier in 1873, it was long confined to the rank of paragon of official art. A recent reinstatement of XIXth century architecture has emphasised the principal ideas prevalent in the building: "classical" in design (symmetrical and axial plan, all elements legible in a building whose purpose and organisation are immediately recognisable) and "baroque" in its decoration (abundance of masks, allegories and detail, diversity of mediums). Easing the tension between order's rationalism and ornamentation's exuberance was the wager won by Garnier, whose masterpiece goes beyond illustrating the eclecticism of the era that witnessed its birth.

Jean-Baptiste Carpeaux

La Danse
(The Dance)

original group for the Opera façade 1866-1869
stone, 420 × 298 cm

Jean-Baptiste Carpeaux (1827-1875) Former student of Rude and winner of the grand Prix de Rome in 1854. The polemic stirred up by his group *Ugolin et ses enfants* (*Ugolin and his Children*) 1859, focused public attention on him. With the imperial family's support, he obtained important commissions (*Flore*, 1863, palais du Louvre, *Les Quatres Parties du Monde* (*The Four Quarters of the World*, 1865-1872, avenue de l'Observatoire) and executed several portraits (*Princess Mathilda*). With *La Danse* (*The Dance*, his most famous work, he reached the peak of his career.

December 1863 witnessed Carpeaux's triumph: he had been chosen to execute one of the large bas-reliefs of the new Opera, under construction since the summer of 1861 and in the hands of Charles Garnier, a friend from youth. The decorative programme foresaw four principal themes: Comedy and Drama, Light and Lyric Poetry, Music and Song, and the Dance of Love and Bacchanalian Dance. Concerned about the harmony of his façade, Garnier imposed a common schema on all the sculptors: each group had to be made up of three characters and a central allegorical figure, a specification noted in the official commission of August 17th, 1865.

In spite of his delicate health, Carpeaux immediately attacked the dance theme. In a mood of feverish creativity, he produced a multitude of sketches, drawings and models, each one more unfaithful to Garnier's indications than the other: one of the studies included up to seventeen figures... The architect resigned himself, realising the originality of the project that finally materialised as a group of nine figures in Echaillon stone: "Well! If the monument suffers a little from my sculptor's exuberance, that will only be a small misfortune, whereas it would be a great one if I stuck to my ideas and deprived France of a work which will surely be a masterpiece."

Carpeaux, who had devoted several years' energy and his fortune to *The Dance*, completed his work in 1869. Installed and unveiled during the summer, it was greeted with scandalised uproar which, on the night of August 26th, led to a group of chaste spirits daubing it with ink that long remained indelible. The bourgeois public would have preferred an ideal or divine allegory to these over "realistic" dancers, these "vulgar characters [who] smell of sweat", denounced by René Ménard in the *Gazette des beaux-arts*. The group was so shocking that the Government was forced to react. The same year, a new commission for a more decent work, meant to replace Carpeaux's group, was given to Gumery. But the war of 1870 intervened. The initial *The Dance* stayed in place until 1964, when, badly damaged by the polluted atmosphere, it was removed to the Louvre, before joining the Orsay Museum's collections. The copy of the sculpture today at the top of the Opéra steps was executed by Paul Belmondo.

Charles Cordier
(1827-1905),
The Negro of Sudan,
1856-1857,
marble, onyx, bronze,
79 cm.

**Sculptural mediums
render service to
illusion: the use of
precious marble and
onyx tones
emphasises the
colour of the bronze.**

Alexandre Falguière
(1831-1900),
*Winner of the
Cockfight*, 1864,
bronze,
174 × 100 cm.

**Renaissance of the
Renaissance: this
slender figure adopts
the running position
of *Mercury* sculpted
by the Italian John of
Bologna.**

Taking advantage of the Second Empire's architectural fever, sculptors actively participated in the decorative programmes of public buildings, especially at the Louvre and in the Tuileries. Sculpture, like painting, was then dominated by the academic system. Though Rude remained an independent master, Jouffroy and Pradier taught at the Ecole des Beaux-Arts. As for Carpeaux, Carrier-Belleuse, Frémiet and Rodin, they attended classes at the School of Drawing and Mathematics, otherwise known as the "Petite Ecole". Here again, Orientalism, in the form of Cordier's African busts started in the 1840s, and the Neoclassical revival, embodied by the conscientious Pradier, won favour with a public equally receptive to Falguière's conventional skills, while Carpeaux's, and later Rodin's, over "realistic" expressivity and ar-

Furniture: Eclecticism
under Napoleon III

François-Désiré Froment-Meurice (1802-1855),
Mirror, 1847
partially gilded silver, painted enamel on copper, translucent enamel on silver, garnets, iron, glass, 130 × 92 × 50.4 cm.
Example of the fashion for historical styles, this ogival Neo-Gothic frame is adorned with the twenty enamelled coats of arms of the former French provinces.

François Eugène Rousseau (1827-1890),
Vase with Tears and Fishes, circa 1878, engraved and painted glass, with inlaid work,
25 × 18 cm.

An example of Japanese influence, this vase was one of the pieces that would later inspire the artists of Art Nouveau and Art Deco.

Imitating, revising, composing: such were the favourite activities of the great cabinet-makers of the Second Empire, like Fourdinois, Grohé, Jenselme and Monbro, who occasionally worked together with famous sculptors and goldsmiths such as Carrier-Belleuse or Barbedienne. This eclecticism, a vague term derived from architecture and philosophy that often has pejorative connotations, in France denotes how different styles were borrowed from, interwoven and reinterpreted in the last half of the XIXth century. Creativity was indeed limited by the popularity of the Neo-Renaissance, Neo-Louis XV and Neo-Louis XVI styles. The latter, also called Louis XVI-Empress, betrayed its love for Marie-Antoinette by copying her taste. But fashion also dictated an ever increasing production due to technical progress (steam planes, mechanised mouldings, electroplating) and to the growing wealth of middle-class families. The forms of the previous century were corrected or copied and then adapted to a new principle: comfort. Upholstery, already found at Versailles in 1708, became widespread and covered pouffes, armchairs, sofas, confidantes (two-seated S-shaped sofas) and "indiscrets" (three-seated helix-shaped sofas). While the Second Empire really invented nothing (not even, as is often thought, papier-mâché furniture inlaid with mother-of-pearl that was already thriving in the Romantic era), it boldly and exuberantly revised history.

Maison Monbro (1807-1884),
Lower Part of a Cabinet, 1855,
ebony, gilded bronze, champlevé enamel and painted enamel on copper, coloured gems, 132 × 86 × 45 cm.
An anthology of references for this cabinet bottom: the bronzes recall Louis XIV and the Regency while the central medallion is Neo-classical.

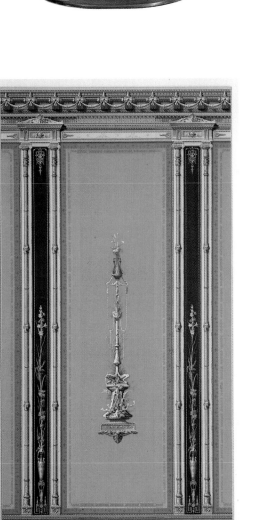

Desfossé and Karth (wallpaper manufacturers) **Neo-Greek style décor,** circa 1867,

A thriving industry under the Second Empire, wallpaper produced here by Jules Desfossé illustrates the new Antiquity craze, at a time when archeological digs discovered colour on ancient monuments.

dour in certain works (*The Dance*) were still considered shocking.

At the same time, artists took advantage of the technical and industrial progress and discoveries made in this era, using and mastering new materials. Goldsmiths like Barbedienne and Christofle discovered the finer points of electroplating that enabled them to produce technical masterpieces. With better tools available, Renaissance or XVIIIth century imitation objets d'art and furniture graced bourgeois dining and drawing rooms: the formal illusion of the past legitimised the fatherless society of worthy men, while technical progress ensured strength and long life.

The infatuation with science spread into art, history and literature. It was present at the birth of photography, an invention both praised and feared, a mirror of the century that left precious evidence of the epoch and its protagonists like the writers and artists captured by Nadar's camera. Photography captured décors and rivalled the delicate watercolours of the drawing room, before earning the status of an art in its own right.

Realism and modernity: the 1863 turning point

Parallel to the upsurge in Republican feeling inspired by the Revolution, which, for equalitarian reasons, had tried to suppress the jury of the 1848 Salon, was the enthusiasm for "lyrical illusion"; these two characteristics marked a whole generation whose most illustrious representatives in the artistic domain remained Gustave Courbet, Honoré Daumier and Jean-François Millet.

As soon as he arrived in Paris in 1840, Courbet scorned the schools. He became leader of the Realist movement by painting contemporary scenes in a style influenced by the Spanish golden age, and on a scale traditionally reserved for great historical works. Slated by the critics for "painting the ugly", he was refused at the 1855 Exposi-

Gustave Courbet (1819-1877),
The Painter's Studio.
True Allegory, 1855,
oil on canvas,
361 × 598 cm.

One of the painter's masterpieces and a huge, planned canvas, "I am in the middle, painting. On the right are the participators, that is to say friends, workers and lovers of the art world. On the left, is the other world of everyday life..." wrote Courbet in 1854.

Jean-François Millet (1814-1875),
The Gleaners, 1857,
oil on canvas,
83 × 111 cm.

Breaking with the idyllic conception of the country, the painter was interested in the reality of rustic life.

Gustave Courbet

Un enterrement à Ornans
(A Burial at Ornans)
(1849-1850)
oil on canvas, 315 × 668 cm

Gustave Courbet
(1819-1877)
Pupil of the Swiss
Academy, Courbet
was passionately
enthusiastic about
the works of
Rembrandt, whom
he studied in 1847,
at the Rijksmuseum
in Amsterdam.
Leader of the Realist
movement,
supported by
Champfleury, he set
up his own pavilion
in 1855 to exhibit his
works rejected at the
Exposition
Universelle. The
density of his
painting, and his use
of everyday or rural
scenes as themes for
monumental
compositions
created a scandal.
A revolutionary
spirit, close to the
philosopher
Proudhon, he was
actively involved in
the Paris Commune
(1871). Arrested and
convicted, he was
exiled to Switzerland
where he spent the
rest of his life.

At the age of thirty, during the summer of 1849, in the attic of the family house at Ornans, Courbet undertook his first monumental work that was his manifesto-painting. His original title, *Tableau de figures humaines, historique d'un enterrement à Ornans* (*Painting of Human Figures, Historical Account of a Burial at Ornans*), effectively illustrates his then radically innovative attempt: to make a historical painting out of an ordinary, country event, elevating everyday reality to the rank of art. Despite the discomfort of his improvised studio ("I'm working blind, I've no backing-space," he wrote to Champfleury), the painter welcomed the inhabitants of Ornans, who were flattered to sit for him: a crowd of nearly fifty, most of whom have today been identified. One can recognise in particular Abbot Bonnet, the village vicar; in the central male group, the mayor Prosper Teste de Sagey and Claude Melchior Proudhon, deputy Justice of the Peace and cousin of the philosopher; and numerous members of the artist's family, such as his three sisters in the guise of mourners, behind the Republican in blue stockings, their mother, holding a young girl by the hand, and of whom this is the only known portrait, and even his grandfather on the far left, who had died a year earlier and to whom this funereal scene paid homage.

Presented at the 1850-1851 Salon, the *Burial* immediately aroused an adverse public reaction, and the critics all slated "this cult of ugliness, this glorification of vulgarity, of odious banality." Among its defenders, however, were Proudhon and Paul Mantz who, in *L'Evénement* of 15th February, 1851, prophesied that this masterpiece would become "in modern history the Hercules'

columns of Realism." *A Burial*, regarded by Courbet as his "début", his "declaration of principles", was above all shocking in its subject's commonplaceness, its scrupulous description, the importance paid to detail in a scene lacking in idealisation and noble aspiration. Rejected at the 1855 Exposition Universelle, but displayed in Realism's independant pavilion, it won no more support.
Requested by the organisers of the 1873 Vienna Exhibition, the work

was finally withdrawn due to the expected outcry. Courbet, then in exile, resigned himself: "The Burial is worthless." Even in 1884, two years after the family had donated it to the Louvre, it was still treated with scorn: "The admission of The Burial to the Louvre is the denial of all aesthetics," proclaimed le Sâr Péladan in *L'Artiste*.
The history of art, however, would eventually accept the painting's capital importance. The theme, once denounced as an anti-clerical manifesto, has also benefited from a remand: in a composition dominated by Christ on the cross – where the clergy, people of all social conditions, a mayor and a freemason judge appear in the same procession – one retains, on the contrary, the idea of a "conciliation" and a "universal entente", one of the constant preoccupations of the XIXth century and especially of the 1848 generation.

Edouard Manet

Olympia

1863
oil on canvas, 130 × 190 cm

Edouard Manet
(1832-1883)
Having started his
career as a naval
officer, Manet
entered the studio of
Thomas Couture,
with whom he
frequently came into
conflict. At the
Louvre, he copied
the Italian, Dutch
and Spanish masters
of the XVIIth and
XVIIIth centuries,
and was later
influenced by
Japanese art. Apart
from an early
success at the 1861
Salon (*Spanish
Guitarist*), his works,
inspired by the great
masters, but treated
in a Naturalist
fashion in order to
depict contemporary
scenes, each time
created an uproar.
His two large works,
*Le Déjeuner sur
l'herbe* (1863) and
Olympia (1865),
mark the beginning
of modern painting.
A friend of the
Impressionists and
close to Zola and
Mallarmé whose
portraits he painted,
he regularly
exhibited in his
studio, away from
the official
exhibition circuit.

On the subject of Edouard Manet's *Olympia* at the 1865 Salon, Jean Ravenel, in his article dated une 2nd in the newspaper *Le Siècle*, stated, "Everyone that passes picks up his stone and throws it in her face." He summed up the reception the vast majority of the public and critics gave the painting: an outrageous idol accompanied by a "hideous negress", *Olympia* "with corpse-like skin" was unanimously rejected.

Yet Manet, who had finished his work in 1863, had evidently delayed showing it after the outcry raised by *Le Déjeuner sur l'herbe*. The painting, which owed its presence at the 1865 Salon to Louis La Caze, the famous collector, and an insistent member of the jury, was intentionally hung on high, above the *Christ insulté* (*Christ Mocked*) by the same artist, so as not to arouse too much protest. Despite these precautions, there were endless comments on the vulgarity of this cold, self-assured prostitute, on her calm arrogance, on the whiteness of her skin, and her nudity exacerbated by the thin, black ribbon around her neck. Not that the nude, an academic subject, was shocking in itself: painters as different as Ingres with *Le Bain turc* (*The Turkish Bath*) and Cabanel with *La Naissance de Vénus* (*The Birth of Venus*) were enormously successful at this time. The anger sprang more from the "manner" used by Manet, who treated the woman's stare with equal importance and as much care as he did her slippers, the cat and the bouquet of flowers. It was the crude "realism" of a contemporary scene, presented without the hierarchy of values, and thus comparable to the first erotic photographs, that shook their awareness. Zola, who in 1867 paid homage to Manet, recognised that this formalism opened the way

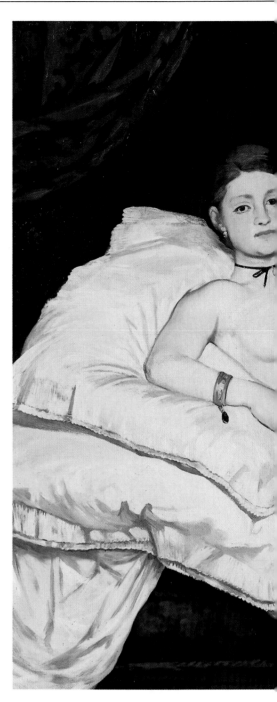

to modernity when he wrote, "This canvas is really the painter's flesh and blood; destiny has indicated its place at the Louvre."
The painting seemed all the more blasphemous in its explicit reference to two famous nudes: Titian's *Venus of Urbino*, from which Manet borrowed the general composition, replacing the servant

by a negress and the pet dog by an ironic, black cat with raised tail, and Goya's *Maja desnuda*, with whose insolence he combines a provocative stare. Finally, to add to the scandal, the 1865 Salon catalogue included under the *Olympia* entry a verse from Astruc's poem that finished with the line, "The majestic maiden who keeps the flame alight," which ultimately classed the painting as a veritable provocation. Consequently, one can see the relevance of Champfleury's comment inspired by *Olympia*, "Like a man who falls over in the snow, Manet has made an impact on public opinion." Discouraged, defeated, Manet took his painting back and kept it till his death. *Olympia* was among the works sold posthumously, but did not reach its reserve price (the minimum amount requested by the seller): it entered the Louvre thanks to Monet's intervention after he launched an appeal fund at the end of 1888.

Edouard Manet
(1832-1883),
*Branch of White
Peonies and
Secateurs,* circa 1864,
oil on canvas,
31 × 46.5 cm.

With this small
painting, framed like
a detail, Manet
suspends time
between the moment
the flowers were cut
and the bouquet was
made.

Henri Fantin-Latour
(1836-1904),
Fruit and Flowers,
1865,
oil on canvas,
64 × 57 cm.

The diagonals of the
painting stand out in
this still-life, while
the presence of the
shortened knife adds
dramatic power.

Henri Regnault
(1843-1871),
*Arbitrary Execution
under the Moorish
Kings of Granada*,
1870,
oil on canvas,
302 × 146 cm.

A late disciple of
Romanticism,
Regnault's work
plays on opposites,
"An intentional
contrast between the
horror of the sinister
act and the
charming gaiety of

his palette," wrote
critic René Ménard
in 1870.

Gustave Moreau
(1826-1898),
Orpheus, 1865,
oil on canvas,
154 × 99 cm.

The memory of
Italian painting is
transferred into a
dreamlike
"somnambulic
world" said André
Breton, where
nature, music and
the passage from life
into death enter into
a whirlwind dance of
correspondences.

tion Universelle: he then grouped his works together in Realism's independant pavilion where he unveiled *L'Atelier du peintre. Allégorie réelle (The Painter's Studio. True Allegory)*, the spectacular manifesto of his theories. This trend, whose rise coincided with a temporary lull in the Romantic movement, swept along Daumier and Millet who applied themselves to depicting work in the fields, as in *Les Botteleurs de foin (The Sheaf Binders)* 1850, *Les Glaneuses (The Gleaners)* 1857, and *The Angelus* (1859).

In this overall climate of both diversity and productivity (the number of exhibits and visitors at the Salons was increasing rapidly), the year 1863 stands out as a landmark: it is generally considered as the year modernity was born. The "Salon des Refusés" started on the 15th May, a fortnight after the official exhibitions opened. The decision to accept the former came from the Emperor, more likely in support of liberalism than the avant-garde. Thus, those rejected by the Salon and disdained by the Institute, could finally present their works in the adjacent rooms laid at their disposal. Among them was Edouard Manet, whose *Le Bain*, *(Bathing)* later known as *Le Déjeuner sur l'herbe (Lunch on the Grass)*, provoked a resounding scandal, together with Henri Fantin-Latour, the American James McNeill Whistler, Camille Pissarro, Dutchman Johan Barthold Jongkind and Henri Harpignies.

At the same time, a few metres away, the Salon was showering praise on Paul Baudry, famous for his monumental compositions in official buildings from the Opéra to the Palais de Justice, Amaury-Duval and Cabanel, whose voluptuous *Venus* with porcelain pink complexion was bought by the Emperor for the Luxembourg Museum. A new generation, however, was taking form behind Manet: that of Degas, Renoir, Bazille and Monet. This avantgarde would mark out the road to Impressionism and be paid homage in Fantin-Latour's group portraits.

Claude Monet
(1840-1926),
The Magpie, circa
1868-1869,
oil on canvas,
89 × 130 cm.

Blue-toned shadows
for this snowscape.
The scale of the
painting is conveyed
by its central feature,
the magpie.

Gustave Guillaumet
(1840-1887),
The Sahara, also
known as
The Desert, 1867,
oil on canvas,
110 × 200 cm.

An Orientalist
canvas from the
"painter traveller"
that tries to capture
an immeasurable
space, integrated
into which is the
image of a carcass:
half-way between
document and
mirage.

Edgar Degas
(1834-1917),
Family Portrait.
The Bellelli Family,
1858-1867,
oil on canvas,
200 × 250 cm.

Set in a bourgeois
interior, it remains a
difficult space to
define: the position
of the characters
together with the
mirror feature
breaks up the
painting's apparently
classical struture.

Daumier
and his incisive genius

Honoré Daumier (1808-1879),
Crispin and Scapin, circa 1864, oil on canvas, 60 × 82 cm.
Daumier transcends the realism of simple
theatrical figures here: under his brush they become
lyrical characters worthy of Goya.

While it is common in the XIXth century to meet artists working simultaneously on sculpture, painting and drawing, rare are those who, like Honoré Daumier (1808-1879), mastered each discipline so brilliantly. He attended the Swiss Academy in Paris, and was a student of Alexandre Lenoir who introduced him to the works of Titian and Rubens. He began his career as a caricaturist in the anti-royalist review *La Caricature* (later called *Le Charivari*), founded by the polemist Charles Philippon in 1831. Daumier's biting line, the scandal and convictions that resulted from the publication of his drawings (six months' prison for his lampoon of Louis-Philippe *Gargantua*) rapidly brought him fame. He also wielded his talent, later recognised by Baudelaire, for handling "this kind of plastic slang" in lithography, and stigmatised magistrates, the middle class, the shabby-genteel and politicians. Used to making models of his subjects before drawing them, Daumier also revealed his skill as a sculptor from 1832 onwards with a series of forty-five busts or "brutalised faces" of right-wing members of parliament.
Bequeathing to the history of engraving and drawing such legendary figures as those of swindler *Robert Macaire* or *Ratapoil,* after 1860 Daumier devoted himself almost exclusively to painting, encouraged by his friends Corot, Millet and Rousseau and admired by Delacroix. His works were characterised by the balance between volume and muted colour, as in *Les Blanchisseuses* or *Le Wagon de 3e classe.*
Blind and destitute at his death, Daumier remains the one outstanding example among his fellow painters of the transition from Romanticism to Realism. He successfully combined theatrical clownery and the sublime, and his prolific output was to have a determinant influence on Manet, Degas and Toulouse-Lautrec.

Honoré Daumier,
*Count Auguste-Hilarion
de Kératry, Deputy,* 1832,
clay, 12 × 12 cm.

The dawning
of Impressionism

At the end of the 1840s, while Realism was in full bloom, numerous artists, influenced by rediscovered English and Dutch XVIIth century works, pointed their research towards landscape painting. Thus, Millet and Théodore Rousseau settled in a village near Fontainebleau, which would give its name to a school that it would be fairer to call a group: Barbizon. Soon joined by Huet, Decamps, Barye, Troyon, Diaz de la Pena, Dupré, Daubigny and even Corot, they took to painting the surrounding countryside "in the open-air", so as to convey, as Millet advocated, "the atmospheric envelope of things." The progressive fragmentaton of brushstrokes and their respect for the fleeting effects of daylight were the innovations later taken up by the Impressionists. Also in this movement were painters like Boudin, who found his inspiration on the Normandy coast and produced seascapes and skies that soon made him famous. Monet, future leader of the Impressionists, often visited him. "If I became a painter, I owe it to Eugène Boudin," he would later say.
Between Normandy and Barbizon, one may find three Dutch artists, Jongkind, the Maris brothers, Jacob and Matthijs, as well as the Frenchman Stanislas Lépine. All of them admired Corot's talent.

Camille Corot (1796-1875),
Boat stranded at Trouville,
1874, oil on canvas, 21 × 23.5 cm.
A tireless traveller, Corot strode through France and Italy
setting up his easel before landscapes where, in his eyes,
light created life.

These artists, whose works were generally rejected by the Salon jury, marked out the road, both in the open-air theme and the technique of separate brushstrokes, for the stars of Impressionism such as Monet and Renoir.

Felix Tournachon, known as Nadar

Portrait of Baudelaire

circa 1855,
print from collodion glass negative,
24 × 17.5 cm

Felix Tournachon,
known as Nadar
(1820-1910)
From 1849 onwards,
he created "Nadar's
Pantheon" in which
he caricatured the
celebrities of the
era, such as Gautier,
Michelet, Doré,
Proudhon, Hugo and
Daudet, using the
photographic
portraits taken in his
workshop. In 1854,
he opened his studio
and became
extremely well-
known.
Journalist and
aerostatics
enthusiast, it is to
him we owe the first
aerial photographs
(he flew over Paris
in a balloon) and the
first pictures taken
in artificial light
(1861). In 1874, the
first Impressionist
exhibition was held
in his studio. In
1900, he published
his photographic
memoirs: *Quand
j'étais photographe.*

Five out of Nadar's twelve portraits of his friend Baudelaire still exist. Among these is one "unsuccessful but sublime", collodion processed print of the poet dressed in black with his hands in his pockets. Tight-mouthed and bitter, his gaze stern, Baudelaire held his pose, staging his own image and probably directing Nadar's willing camera himself. The "blurred" effect that gives the picture its sudden and terrible truth was due to the long exposure time required by collodion, up to twenty seconds. An identical, but sharper, photograph leads one to think that this was a trial attempt before the final print. Nevertheless, the picture, somehow unintentionally complying with the poet's desire for an "accurate" portrait "but with the softness of a drawing", when he wanted his mother photographed in 1865, fleetingly captures the meeting of two essential personalities of the XIXth century. First, Baudelaire who, in his 1859 essay *Salon*, slated the new invention in these terms, "From that moment on, vile society rushed, as one Narcissus, to contemplate its trivial image on a metal plate." Miraculously, Nadar seemed to escape Baudelaire's criticisms, and the poet dedicated *Le Rêve d'un curieux* to him. The photographer, also interested in science and anatomy, from which he derived part of his knowledge on facial expression, was sensitive to "the moral intelligence" of his models who included Baudelaire and numerous other literary and artistic celebrities of the era. "The heads that Nadar photographed around 1860 have long been dead. But their gaze remains, and through their gaze the world of the Second Empire [remains] eternally present," Jean-Paul Sartre was to say.

Baudelaire and Zola, writers and critics

Much more than men of letters acting as Salon chroniclers, Baudelaire and Zola, Diderot's worthy successors, played the role of true art critics. Their pertinent judgement and analysis opened the way masterfully to the understanding of XIXth century aesthetics. This proved an even more valuable lesson as Baudelaire died in 1867, and Zola wrote his first Salon review in 1866; a mere chronological coincidence that would be tempting, but fallacious, to see in terms of a relay, so different were their respective ideas.

Baudelaire confessed early to his "cult of images, (my grand, my unique, my primitive passion)" that, together with his poetic works, belong to the great adventure in which he was involved. He denounced at one and the same time the pure formalism, the sermonising moralism of academic and Realist painters, and the utilitarianism of painting. He refuted "chance in art as in mechanics," to defend an ideal based on curiosity, vigilance, imagination "the queen of one's faculties," and the revelation of modernity. Above all Baudelaire admired Delacroix, the absolute master he had met the first year he wrote *Salon*, in 1845, whose genius he never stopped praising, and Constantin Guys "the painter of modern life." He loved the exotic dream expressed in Fromentin's paintings, like *La Chasse au faucon* (*Hawking*) in Algeria, but slated "the foolish nature cult" in landscape painting or works like Millet's *Les Glaneuses* (*The Gleaners*). He encouraged and helped Manet, Daumier and Meryon.

Baudelaire's avowed preference for painting, drawing (which he practised himself) and engraving led him to judge sculpture and photography severely. Nevertheless, his strikingly acute and contemporary essays on Romanticism, caricature and comedy in art laid the theoretical basis for a definition of modernity.

If for Baudelaire "beauty is always bizarre," for Zola, a work of art was "a corner of creation seen through a temperament" a definition the writer measured the effect of in the works of Courbet and Manet in particular. But though the author of *les Rougon-Macquart* passionately defended young talent against academicism, he waited all his life for "the artistic genius who would produce the new formula," the leader of a Naturalist school of painting, the role he himself held in literature. Condemning "M. Cabanel's toilet powder," and speaking ironically about a Meissonier whose talent was limited to "being clever and looking pretty," Zola was, however, mistrustful of the Impressionists and their swift technique, but prophesied all the same, "The future is there." After long years of absence from art criticism, in 1898 he wrote for the last time on Rodin's statue of Balzac. It was the year of the Dreyfus Affair and the famous "I accuse," in which Zola definitively establishes himself as an artist committed on all fronts.

Edouard Manet (1832-1883),
Emile Zola, 1868,
oil on canvas, 146.3 × 114 cm.

head inset:
caricature of Baudelaire by Manet

Essays by Charles Baudelaire on painting: *Curiosités esthétiques, L'art romantique* in 1868.
Essays by Emile Zola: *Ecrits sur l'art* followed by *Manet* in 1867.

ITINERARY

'3

Exploration

■ Manet, a confirmed Impressionist?
■ Degas, a singular artist
■ When light became "pastel"
■ For or against the Impressionists?
■ A doctor in attendance
■ The Caillebotte Affair
■ Japanism

Discoveries

■ Monet's decorative panel *Le Déjeuner*
■ Renoir's *Dance at the Moulin de la Galette*
■ Degas' *Little Dancer of Fourteen*
■ Emile Bernard's *Madeleine in the Bois d'Amour*
■ Van Gogh's *The Painter's Room at Arles*
■ Gauguin's *The Beautiful Angèle*

Encounter with

■ Etienne Moreau-Nélaton, collector

The Impressionist Line (1870-end of the century)

by Marina Ferretti-Bocquillon

The 1870s witnessed both the coming of the IIIrd Republic and the evolution of Impressionism. Led by their friend Monet, Pissarro, Sisley and Renoir looked afresh at landscape and expressed the most fleeting effects of light. Thanks to the new exhibition and sales circuits, and a few clairvoyant critics and art dealers who spoke in their defence, the Impressionists aroused the enthusiasm of a small number of buyers. The 1880s saw growing divergence within the movement: such different personalities as Seurat, Gauguin, Van Gogh and Toulouse-Lautrec found themselves next to the Neo-Impressionists, the Pont-Aven school and the Nabis.

The Orsay Museum's Impressionist collections come mainly from the former Jeu de Paume Museum. They have been enriched by such key works as Sérusier's *The Talisman* and Monet's *The Magpie*, and works by artists rarely shown or otherwise absent from the Jeu de Paume, like Bonnard and the Nabis, the Neo-Impressionists or Gauguin as a sculptor.

1870

Declaration of the Franco-Prussian War and defeat on December 2nd at Sedan. Bazille killed in action. Proclamation of the IIIrd Republic. Monet and Pissarro visited London and met dealer Durand-Ruel.

1871

France lost the War. Fighting in Paris under the Commune. Monet moved to Argenteuil.

1873

New "Salon des Refusés."

1874

First Impressionist Exhibition at Nadar's studio.

1875

Inauguration of the Opéra de Paris.

1876

The Impressionist Exhibition held at Durand-Ruel's. Work started on the construction of the Sacré-Coeur in Montmartre.

1878

Cézanne settled in the South of France.

1882

Invention of Synthetism by Gauguin and Emile Bernard at Pont-Aven.

1883

Death of Manet.

1884

Birth of the Salon des Artistes Indépendants whose maxim was "no jury, no prize," in Paris. Foundation of the artists' collective, known as Les XX, in Brussels.

1886

Van Gogh arrived in Paris. Eighth and last Impressionist Exhibition without Monet, Renoir, Cézanne or Sisley. Durand-Ruel organised an Impressionist Exhibition in New York. Jean Moréas published the *Manifeste du symbolisme*.

1888

On Gauguin's instructions, Sérusier painted *The Talisman*: birth of the Nabis.

1889

The Paris Exposition Universelle: inauguration of the Eiffel Tower. Opening of the Moulin-Rouge where Lautrec's works were on view.

1890

Van Gogh committed suicide at Auvers-sur-Oise.

1891

Gauguin left for Tahiti. Death of Seurat. First exhibition devoted to the Nabis at the Galerie Le Barc de Boutteville.

1894

Assassination of Sadi Carnot, President of the Republic. Following the wave of anarchist bomb attacks, Luce and Fénéon were implicated in the trial of the thirty suspected terrorists.

1895

First film projection given by the Lumière brothers in Paris.

1897

Viennese *Sezession*.

At the dawn of the IIIrd Republic, France had changed. It had experienced defeat at Sedan and the tragic events of the Commune, but the industrialisation policy pushed through by Napoleon IIIrd had borne its fruit. Paris had been transfigured under Haussmann's administration. The railway encouraged the growth of tourism; travelling and holidays in the country or on the Normandy coast were no longer reserved for a privileged élite or the occasional eccentric. The middle classes took full advantage of the economic boom during the Second Empire; they enjoyed Sundays in the country, boating parties, bathing and walks along the Seine.

As for the painters, they ardently observed this new landscape, crisscrossed by trains and railway bridges, with the odd factory chimney in sight now and again. Nature stopped playing its background role to historical or mythological deeds, as in the paintings of Bouguereau, Delaunay and Henner. As early as the 1860s, Monet, Renoir and Sisley left Gleyre's studio, where they had first met, to paint in Fontainebleau forest. There, they rediscovered the haunts of Corot, Daubigny and Rousseau.

Argenteuil: 1872-1878, the heroic years

The geography of Impressionism can be mapped out along the water. From Paris and its suburbs to the Normandy coast, it follows the flow of the Seine through Argenteuil, Vétheuil, Giverny, Vernon and Rouen, with a slight detour via Pontoise and Auvers-sur-Oise to include Pissarro and Cézanne. Argenteuil, situated on the banks of the Seine, about ten kilometres west of Paris, was the movement's favourite spot. In 1870, Parisians had started going there by train or boat: in twenty minutes and for a few francs, they could watch the river ballet in a setting that was still rustic.

Monet moved to Argenteuil at the end of

Claude Monet
1840-1926),
Régates à Argenteuil
(*Sailing Boats*
at Argenteuil),
circa 1872,
oil on canvas,
48 × 75 cm.

Reality and its
reflection. An
epitome of Monet's
art and his
fascination for water.

1871. He stayed there six years and was often visited by Manet, whose family house was nearby in Gennevilliers, also home of Caillebotte; It was here that Manet painted his most Impressionist works, *Argenteuil* and *En Bateau* (*Boating*). Their friend Renoir was another frequent visitor, as was Sisley who lived in Sèvres. Monet had fitted out a boat as a floating studio, in Argenteuil, and painted some one hundred and seventy-five canvases, among the most brilliant of his works. The Argenteuil basin, the boating parties and regattas, the railway bridge and footbridge inspired a profusion of masterpieces from the Impressionist group. Despite the overwhelming material difficulties that beset the majority of the artists, these paintings remain the most radiant, the most resplendent of their production.

The Impressionist painters were still in their youth; they had defined a new style and were working side by side. There was no talk of a school, since they had published no common manifesto, nor established an original theory of painting, except that of observing the world around them and expressing its most fleeting aspects. United in their mutual admiration for Courbet, Turner and Constable, they radicalised the trends of their immediate predecessors, Daubigny, Jongkind and Boudin. Using assertive brushstrokes and light colours, they extolled the virtues of working outside, made easier by the recent invention of tubes of paint that enabled them to paint on the spot in the open air. They concentrated on conveying the variations in light, which forced them to work swiftly, to simplify their compositions and to fragment their brushwork.

After the defeat at Sedan and the dramatic outcome of the Commune, the works of the Argenteuil period captured the image of a radiant, cloudless suburb, devoted to the pleasures of Parisians' leisure time; if the occasional factory chimney could be seen smoking on the horizon, it betrayed nothing of the radical transformation industrialisation was soon to inflict on this site. Travelling west meant passing through Saint-Lazare Station that caught the attention of Manet and Caillebotte; as for Monet, he dedicated a whole series of paintings to it, in flamboyant homage to the locomotive bellowing clouds of steam.

Salons and dealers: the new system

For the Impressionists, getting known, exhibiting their works and making a meagre living, was like running an obstacle race. From the end of the 1860s, the Pre-Impressionists' paintings no longer met with academic requirements, and were systematically rejected by the jury in charge of selecting works to be displayed at the Salon: the most important artistic event of the year, it attracted a large public and art critics covered it in detail. True, a few courageous dealers like Durand-Ruel or Martinet exhibited their non-academic artists, but the impact of these shows remained limited.

Even before the Impressionists, painters had already defied this sacrosanct institution. First Courbet, who set up, outside the 1855 Exposition Universelle, a booth proudly baptised "Realism's Pavilion", in which he displayed his rejected canvases. In spite of his lack of success, he repeated the experience during the 1867 Exposition Universelle. This time, he was not alone: Manet also opened a private exhibition, near the Pont de l'Alma. It was not the first time Manet was involved in a scandal. *Le Déjeuner sur l'herbe* had caused an outcry four years earlier, at the "Salon des Refusés" opened on Napoleon III's initiative.

For their part, Monet and his friends chose to organise the presentation of their works to the public personally. In 1874, the first exhibition of paintings from the "Batignolles group" was held in the photographer Nadar's studio in the boulevard des Capucines. It caused a sensation and was a financial flop for the artists who had mounted the

Edouard Manet (1832-1883), *Stéphane Mallarmé,* 1876, oil on canvas, 27.5 × 36 cm.

The antithesis of *Zola's* rigid pose, this is the most Impressionist of Manet's portraits and one that he gave to his model the poet.

Berthe Morisot (1841-1895), *La Chasse aux papillons (The Butterfly Hunt),* 1874, oil on canvas, 46 × 56 cm.

Harmony in green and white. Manet's pupil and sister-in-law, Berthe Morisot took part in the Impressionist Exhibitions from 1874 onwards and organised the one held in 1886.

Claude Monet

Claude Monet (1840-1926) Monet spent his youth in Le Havre, where he worked in the open air with Boudin and met Jongkind. In 1862 he entered Gleyre's studio in Paris, and became friends with Renoir and Sisley, whom he coaxed into painting outside in Fontainebleau forest. He lived in Argenteuil from 1871-1878 (*Le Pont de chemin de fer à Argenteuil – The Railway Bridge at Argenteuil*, around 1873-1874), then moved to Vétheuil (*Vétheuil, view from Lavacourt*, 1879). In 1883, he settled permanently in Giverny (*Femme à l'ombrelle – Woman with a Parasol*, 1886). He travelled extensively in Italy, Holland and London. From 1890 onwards, he set up a new studio and worked on his garden, later creating his water garden (*Le Bassin aux nymphéas; harmonie verte – The Waterlily Pool; Harmony in Green*, 1899) that he never tired of painting until his death.

Le Déjeuner
(Lunch)

circa 1873
oil on canvas, 160 × 201 cm.

From *Femmes au jardin* (*Women in a Garden*), 1867, to *Nymphéas* (*Waterlilies*) whose tones the artist analysed for the last thirty years of his life, Monet's favourite themes remained flowers, gardens and the study of water and its reflections. This view of the artist's garden in Argenteuil stands out from his other paintings of this period. Monet had momentarily forsaken large-scale works, hardly conducive to painting in the open air, where priority was given to landscape, and human figures were often limited to vague outlines. Here, on the contrary, the painter's son, Jean, is entirely recognisable in the foreground on the left.

But Monet's concessions to what he called "museum art" stopped there. He pushed the figures back to the edge of the painting: the child is shadowed by the luncheon table, while the womens' two thin silhouettes blend into the front of the house and the flowerbeds. Their dresses add a splash of light to the background, but they are nothing more than a distant memory of *Femmes au jardin* (*Women in a Garden*) painted in 1867.

In this elaborate composition, Monet calmly and boldly centred attention on the splendid still-life in the foreground. His main preoccupation was to depict the spots of sunlight invading the garden and the abandoned lunch table. The brightness of the cloth, the transparency of the glasses, and the warm tones of the fruit help create this dazzling evocation of a sunny spring day. The atmosphere of this scene from daily life, the family meal, is also conveyed by the odd detail: a serviette left on the table, a straw hat carelessly hung on the branch of the lilac tree. There is no sky, no horizon, not even a path to break up the space; the housefront blocks one's view and enhances the intimacy of the scene. The composition is built around the alternate zones of light and shade, the analysis of which so preoccupied the painter. The memory of classical perspective lingers in the line of the wicker trolley and the bench with the umbrella and adds an illusion of depth to the canvas. Beyond the obvious charm of this work, *Le Déjeuner* was the forerunner of the large, decorative panels Bonnard and Vuillard would execute twenty years later.

Manet,
a confirmed Impressionist?

For or against
the Impressionists?

Judgement was passed, the critics were unanimous: *Le Déjeuner sur l'herbe* opened the way for the Impressionists. It would soon be the turn of these painters to adopt contemporary themes and a freedom of treatment that would take them further than Manet. At a time when "modern painting" meant "Impressionism", it was logical to consider Manet as an Impressionist painter. This was, however, forgetting Manet's than those of the Impressionists: Manet was not a landscape painter; he was unconcerned by capturing on the spot the fleeting effects of light and his compositions remained highly complex. Furthermore, Manet never denied classical painting and often produced modern versions of its themes. This is especially noticeable in *The Balcony* and *Lola of Valence*, both freely inspired by Goya's works. Without denying the past, Ma-

Edouard Manet, *On the Beach*, 1873,
oil on canvas, 59.5 × 73 cm.
Even when Manet, like the Impressionists, worked in the open air (sand was found in his paint), landscape stayed in the background.

ambiguous attitude: he systematically refused to take part in the Impressionists' Exhibitions and chose to submit his paintings to the Salon, his work remaining very different from that of his friends. If we leave aside a few famous paintings like *Argenteuil* or *Boating*, the artist of *Olympia* and *The Balcony* had other preoccupations net's approach sometimes led him directly to the threshold of the XXth century. In one light step *The Fife Player* of 1886 jumped several decades: Its radical spareness and visual impact were forerunners of Gauguin and Matisse's research. For Manet, Impressionism was not a compulsory stepping-stone on the road to modernity.

Edouard Manet (1832-1883), *Asparagus*, 1880,
oil on canvas, 16 × 21.5 cm.
Nothing...or almost nothing: a few brushstrokes, three dabs of colour make a yellow and violet asparagus into a most surprising still-life.

The critics were hostile when Romanticism emerged and slated the growing Realist movement. The 1874 Exhibition aroused another wave of protestation. It was Louis Leroy, a reviewer for *Charivari*, a satirical magazine, that coined the term "Impressionism" in a scathing attack on Monet's *Impression, Sunrise*, on view at Nadar's studio in 1874. The critic Albert Wolff of the *Figaro* was the most virulent. The 1867 Exhibition, according to him, presented "five or six lunatics, including a woman" (naturally, he was speaking of the Impressionists and Berthe Morisot). "Try explaining to Mr. Renoir that a woman's torso is not a heap of decomposing flesh, covered in green and purplish bruises..," he ranted. He later deplored that a man "such as Mr. Degas [tarried] in this mass of nonentities."
Luckily, the Batignolles group had found a few critics more receptive to their art. Duranty, Théodore Duret, Philippe Burty, and later Octave Mirbeau, Gustave Geffroy and Félix

Fénéon admired, analysed, defended their works and convincingly demonstrated the historical importance of Impressionism.
Among their defenders were several of the group's friends and many writers: poets like Jules Laforgue, Emile Verhaeren and Stéphane Mallarmé and novelists like Joris-Karl Huysmans. The latter was one of the first to defend Cézanne; he also found in the works of Manet and Degas the echo of his own Naturalist tendencies. When his writings veered towards Symbolism, he evidently turned to the works of Redon and Moreau: his description of Gustave Moreau's *Salomé* remains one of the most beautiful passages in his book *A rebours*. The painters also cast a perceptive glance at the works of their contemporaries: "Monet has an eye, the most prodigious eye since painters came into existence [...] He will go to the Louvre, next to Constable and Turner," said Cézanne at the end of the century.

Caricature by **Cham,**
in *Le Charivari*, 1877
*"Madam! That would be most imprudent.
Please go away!"*

Alfred Sisley
(1839-1899),
La Barque pendant l'inondation, Port-Marly, (*Boat in the Flood, Port-Marly*),
1876,
oil on canvas,
50.5 × 61 cm.

For Sisley, the flood provides another opportunity to analyse the effects of light.

Paul Cézanne
(1839-1906),
Le Pont de Maincy, près de Melun, (*The Bridge at Maincy, near Melun*), 1879,
oil on canvas,
58.5 × 72.5 cm.

Cézanne's preoccupation with geometry is evident here. The dense, static water acts as a mirror.

Emile Bernard

Emile Bernard
(1868-1941)
Painter, poet and art
critic, he was
originally a student
in Cormon's studio
where he met
Toulouse-Lautrec,
van Gogh and
Anquetin. He
invented Synthetism
with Gauguin in
1888 at Pont-Aven
(*La Moisson – The
Harvest*, 1888) and
exhausted himself
claiming its
paternity, while
moving towards a
more mystical art
form. He travelled in
Italy and Egypt
where he stayed
eleven years. On his
return in 1904, he
settled in Aix near
Cézanne. In 1907, he
published their
correspondence and
conversations in the
Mercure de France.
He then devoted
himself to an art
form inspired by
classical and even
academic painting
(*Après le bain, Les
Nymphes – After
Bathing, The
Nymphs*, 1908).

Madeleine au bois d'Amour
(Madeleine in the Bois d'Amour)
1888,
oil on canvas, 138 × 163 cm

Madeleine au bois d'Amour is without question Emile Bernard's masterpiece. The twenty-year-old artist had just invented Synthetism with Gauguin, in opposition to the analytical approach adopted by the Impressionists. The two friends were soon to enter into a dispute over the paternity of this art form that also owes a lot to Cézanne. Synthetism, sometimes called cloisonnism because of its use of black outlines as in stained-glass windows, was intended to be more evocative than descriptive. Flat areas of matt colour were applied and outlined in dark blue: only essential forms and colour were retained.

The wood known as the Bois d'Amour, near Pont-Aven, had already inspired Gauguin two years earlier; it was there he instructed Sérusier, in October 1888, to paint a famous landscape that the latter would carry preciously back to his friends at the Julian academy in Paris: *The Talisman*, now on display at the Orsay Museum.

The young woman who lies dreaming and after whom the painting was named, was Madeleine Bernard, the artist's sister. She was seventeen and spent the summer at Pont-Aven. She was beautiful, and had just met Gauguin who asked her to pose for a portrait, today in the Museum of Grenoble. The landscape is simplified to the extreme: no sky, horizontality of the River Aven whose still waters reflect the foliage, verticality of the tree trunks. In the foreground, Madeleine, like a recumbent figure on a tombstone, lies stiff and immobile as the water, and occupies the whole length of the canvas. The only volume is in the young girl's face. Radically different from the seductive nymphs of academic art, from Renoir's voluptuous bathers or from Monet's modern young women enjoying a picnic, Madeleine recalls the Symbolist universe. Chaste and contemplative, she becomes the priestess in a timeless, sacred wood. After Puvis de Chavannes came a wave of mystical and utopic visions of landscape. This taste for depicting an ideal landscape may be found in such varied works as Henri Cross' *L'Air du soir* (*Evening Breeze*), 1893, Maurice Denis' *Le Jeu de volant* (*The Game of Shuttlecock*), 1900, and even Rousseau's *The Snake Charmer* in 1907.

show at their own expense. But they had acted as a coherent movement, and had been accidentally baptised "Impressionists" by critic Louis Leroy in his ironic lines on Monet's *Impression, Soleil levant* (*Impression,Sunrise*), "Impression, I was sure of it. I also told myself, since I'm impressed, there must be an impression there somewhere...[...] And what freedom, what ease in the treatment! Wallpaper in its embryonic state has a better finish than that seascape." Impressionism, born a few years earlier, now had a name, and the eight "Impressionist Exhibitions" that were held from 1874 to 1886 set the pace for the movement's evolution. In 1876, exhibitors were asked to submit to one condition: no presentation of works to the Salon jury. Their shows were not to be considered, under any pretext, as a "Refusés" exhibition: they were deliberately organised outside official circuits.

Soon, other shows helped to demolish the Paris Salon's importance, and Durand-Ruel launched the era of the art dealer. Ten years after the first Impressionist Exhibition, 1884 saw the birth of the Salon des Artistes Indépendants whose maxim was "no jury, no prize", and where the real end of the century innovations would be shown. Brussels also appeared on the international artistic scene with the Les XX, and later, the Libre Esthétique exhibitions.

New sales networks sprung up outside of conventional circuits thanks to the initiative taken by a few people with highly individual taste. Paul Durand-Ruel met Monet and Pissarro in London in 1870; from then on, he courageously gave them his support. He helped organise the 1874 exhibition, and held the one in 1876 in his own gallery. After having exhibited the Impressionists in Rotterdam, Berlin and London, in 1886 he set out to conquer the American market and mounted a show in New York. He was assisted by the painter Mary Cassatt who convinced her wealthy compatriots to invest in her friends' works. Other smaller dealers also encouraged the Impressionist painters:

Mary Cassatt (1844-1926), *Woman Sewing in a Garden,* circa 1880-1882, oil on canvas, 92 × 63 cm.

Women and children made up American Mary Cassatt's essential repertoire. Her incisive line and original compositions compelled Degas' admiration.

Pierre-Auguste Renoir (1841-1919), *Etude. Torse, effet de soleil* (*Study. Nude in the Sunlight*), circa 1875-1876, oil on canvas, 81 × 65 cm.

Immersed in nature, a woman's torso shaded in blue and the occasional touch of colour. At the second Impressionist Exhibition in 1876, it caused a scandal.

Pierre-Auguste Renoir (1841-1919), *La Balançoire (The Swing)*, 1876, oil on canvas, 92 × 73 cm.

Like *The Dance at the Moulin de la Galette, The Swing* recalls the happy moments at the height of Impressionism.

Pierre-Auguste Renoir

Bal du moulin de la Galette, Montmartre

(Dance at the Moulin de la Galette, Montmartre)

1876, oil on canvas, 131 × 175 cm

Pierre-Auguste Renoir (1841-1919) A porcelain painter, Renoir entered Gleyre's studio in 1862 and met Monet, with whom, at the end of the 1880s, he laid out the road to Impressionism. He broke away from the movement in 1883, after a journey to Italy, and went back to a more classical art form (*Les Grandes Baigneuses – The Bathers*, 1885, exhibited in the Philadelphia Museum). He settled in Cagnes in 1903, and from then on used red tones in his paintings as in *Gabrielle à la rose* (*Gabrielle with Rose*),1911. The Orsay Museum's famous *Baigneuses* (*The Bathers*) were painted in 1919, the last year of his life.

One of the major works of both Renoir and Impressionism, the *Dance at the Moulin de la Galette* held pride of place in Gustave Caillebotte's collection. He even went as far as to reproduce it in an *Auto-Portrait*. The intoxicating atmosphere of the Moulin de la Galette, one of the last Parisian open air dance halls, had made it popular. At the foot of the windmill that still exists, people from Montmartre's lower middle classes would go there to relax and enjoy themselves on Sundays. Toulouse-Lautrec also left us his interpretation of the dance at the Moulin de la Galette: nocturnal and confined, it is radically different from this one.

Renoir, whose studio was in nearby rue Corot, was a regular patron and it was here that he chose to depict his painter, model and critic friends. Another smaller version of this canvas also exists. Whether it was a study or a replica, it proves that Renoir attached special importance to this work, perhaps the most ambitious of his Impressionist period. Georges Rivière, Renoir's biographer and friend, appears on the right of the canvas which, according to him, was entirely painted outside. It is, however, difficult to imagine that the work was really done on the spot: its dimensions would have complicated the undertaking and a composition involving so many characters is not easily improvised. *The Dance at the Moulin de la Galette* has been compared to Ruben's *Kermesse* and Watteau's *L'Embarquement pour Cythère* (*Embarkation for Cythera*), which the artist could have seen in the Louvre. Beyond the dance theme and the embracing couple, there is a similarity in the composition. Renoir's follows a curve that starts at the figures sitting down on the right, then passes through the young woman standing in the foreground and the dancing couples that draw one's gaze to the crowd at the back of the painting. To give the effect of a rapid glance at the scene, while emphasising the atmosphere of lively disorder, Renoir readily crops some of the figures.

The colour distribution very subtly conceals this elaborate composition under a veil of blue and pink. The glint of sunlight filtering through the acacia trees, the shadows and the mens' dark blue suits, the absence of black and grey, and the sketchy background figures all help to convey the gay atmosphere of the dance. Renoir was later to interpret this theme very differently in his panels *La Danse à la Ville* (*Dance in the City*) and *La Danse à la Campagne* (*Dance in the Country*): henceforth each couple would be isolated, greater attention would be paid to draughtsmanship, with discreet shadows and fewer colours as the artist distanced himself from Impressionism.

Martinet, Georges Petit and Père Martin. The most picturesque figure was the artists' supplier Père Tanguy who accepted payment in paintings. His shop was for a long time one of the rare places in Paris where Cézanne's canvases could be admired.

A certain number of art lovers also played an essential role in the painters' lives. Publisher Georges Charpentier, whose writers included Flaubert, Zola, Maupassant and the Goncourts, supported Renoir. The baritone Faure bought Manet's canvases, while Monet's were bought by the financier Hoschédé. As for the painter Caillebotte, he guaranteed a place for his friends' works in the museum by bequeathing his collection to the State. Finally, Dr. Gachet lodged Cézanne and Guillaumin in his house at Auvers-sur-Oise, before helping van Gogh during the last months of his life.

The breakup of Impressionism: the years 1880-1886

The Impressionist group had formed in the 1860s through chance meetings at the studio. It broke up at the beginning of the 1880s. From then on, Cézanne spent more and more time in the south; Monet settled permanently in Giverny in 1883. The following year, Pissarro left Pontoise for Eragny. Sisley had abandoned Sèvres for the outskirts of Moret. Renoir remained a resident of Paris, but travelled in Algeria and Italy, where he admired the works of Raphaël. The seventh Impressionist Exhibition in 1882 was in fact the last time the painters acted as a coherent group. Each member then became more involved in personal research and some even questioned the validity of Impressionism: Renoir's feelings were divided when he admitted he had reached "the end of Impressionism." Tired of painting "as the bird sings," he looked back and took note from Ingres: his panels, *La Danse à la ville* (*Dance in the City*) and *La Danse à la campagne* (*Dance in the Country*), illus-

Camille Pissarro (1830-1903), *Gelée blanche (Hoar Frost)*, 1873, oil on canvas, 65 × 93 cm.

A scant landscape, with little thought to composition. The trees' oblique shadows fall on the frozen furrows, and bring a necessary strength to the frozen landscape.

Georges Seurat (1859-1891), *Poseuse de dos (Model from Behind)*, 1887, oil on wood, 24.5 × 15.5 cm.

Behind the blue-mauve brushstrokes, the body seems to fade into space, blurring the image of the model in the same pose as Ingres' *Baigneuse Valpinçon* (*Woman Bathing*).

Georges Seurat
(1859-1891),
Le Cirque
(***The Circus***), 1891,
oil on canvas,
185.5 × 152.5 cm.

**Charmed by the
lights, colours and
animated grace of
the performance,
Seurat contrasts the
artificial gaiety of the
ring with the static
space of the stands.**

**Henri de Toulouse-
Lautrec** (1864-1901),
La Danse mauresque
or *La Goulue en
almée* (***The Moorish
Dance*** or ***La Goulue
as an Arab Dancing
Girl***),
one of the two panels
decorating La
Goulue's stall at the
Foire du Trône, 1895,
oil on canvas,
298 × 316 cm.

**With this work–
painting, poster or
fairground sign–
Toulouse-Lautrec
praised the talent of
his friend La Goulue.**

Eva Gonzales
(1849-1883),
*Une Loge aux
Italiens* (***A Box at the
Théatre des Italiens***),
circa 1874, oil on
canvas,
98 × 130 cm.

**Paris under the
Second Empire
thrived on all forms
of entertainment
from opera to the
"café-concert". The
fashionable elegance
of the people in the
box was a show in
itself.**

When light became "pastel"

trate his renewed interest in composition and drawing. In Giverny, Monet foresaw the risk of falling into a repetitive academicism. With his two canvases entitled *Femme à l'ombrelle* (*Woman with a Parasol*) he returned to large-scale figurative painting, which he had given up several years earlier. Imperceptibly, his work evolved and, without admitting it, he abandoned the Impressionist credo: painting from nature in the open air and capturing the immediacy of light effects. He worked patiently on his garden, which he composed like a painting, and then started to paint endless *Nymphéas* (*Waterlilies*), each one more lyrical and less "objective" and heralding the boldest approach to painting at the beginning of the XXth century.

Cézanne had long since decided to make Impressionism into "something solid like museum art." As for Pissarro, he turned towards younger artists and embarked on the Neo-Impressionist adventure.

1886: the year everything changed

The eighth and last Impressionist Exhibition was held in 1886 and given the very sober title of *8th Painting Exhibition*: it was hard to speak of Impressionism since Monet, Renoir, Sisley and Cézanne were no longer present. Of the original circle, only Camille Pissarro remained, but he had temporarily abandoned the rapid, spontaneous, Impressionist technique for the "exact technique" of a group of young painters exhibiting as a coherent movement for the first time: the Neo-Impressionists. Seurat, Signac, Camille Pissarro and his son Lucien had reserved the last room to present their canvases which were distinctive in the use of tiny dotted brushstrokes. That year it was the young Seurat's work *Un dimanche après-midi à la grande Jatte* (*Sunday Afternoon at the Grande Jatte*), that created a sensation. Degas was present; he had insisted on Forain and Zandomeneghi, who

Despite their fragility, being difficult to fix and sensitive to both light and vibrations, pastels were immensely successful in the XIXth century, and the Orsay Museum devotes several rooms to them. Artists from Delacroix to Redon let themselves be tempted by this technique, which combined the instant charm of its dry, brilliant colours with the spontaneity of drawing. Thanks to a water-based medium, its pigments re-

in colour research. Millet had already seen it in this light: the *Bouquet de marguerites* (*Bouquet of Daisies*) was not a hymn to the virtues of rural life, but simply a luminous study of flowers. While Manet followed brilliantly in the portrait tradition, frequently using a bold treatment absent from his canvases, Degas remained the greatest innovator in pastel. He experimented with new mixes: oil for unctuosity or turpentine to ob-

Edgar Degas (1834-1917),
Fin d'arabesque (End of Arabesque), 1876-1877,
"peinture à l'essence" and pastel, 67 × 38 cm.
Degas willingly mixed techniques. Here the yellow, white and blue hints of pastel literally illuminate the matt tones of the stage.

tain all their brightness and give the coloured surface a slightly velvety, powdered aspect.

Reinstated by the XVIIIth century portraitists, the art of pastel was also appreciated for its elegant execution, a certain worldly brio whose echo is found in Helleu's works. With its infinitely varied colour range, it above all offered artists of the last half of the XIXth century a vast field of exploration

tain a stronger matt effect. By the end of his life, he had attained a chromatism of exceptional intensity. The immaterial quality conveyed by pastel also fascinated the Symbolists who were preoccupied with dreams and introspection. When Odilon Redon took up pastels at the end of the century, his colours were imbued with a suggestive magic and the powdery aspect of his works was strikingly modern.

Henri de Toulouse-Lautrec (1864-1901), *Rousse (La Toilette) – Red-head (Washing)*, 1889, "peinture à l'essence" on cardboard, 67 × 54 cm.

A pale yellow light falls on the young woman's hair and delicate neck.

Henri-Edmond Cross (1856-1910), *La Chevelure (Hair)*, circa 1892, oil on canvas, 61 × 46 cm.

Hair overflows onto the surface of the canvas and surrenders to the Neo-Impressionist abstract play of small dots.

Edgar Degas (1834-1917), *Le Tub (The Tub)*, 1886, pastel, 60 × 83 cm.

A modern version of Diana bathing or the biblical Suzanne, a woman washing provides a fitting subject for the modern nude. Degas' gaze is non-complacent.

Berthe Morisot (1841-1895), *Jeune femme se poudrant (Young Woman Powdering Her Face)*, 1877, oil on canvas, 46 × 39 cm.

One of the numerous Impressionist interpretations of the woman dressing theme. Here, the artist has taken advantage of the delicate monochrome painting formed by the dressing-gown, the curtain and the mirror's reflection.

were not at all Impressionist, taking part in the show. But another "newcomer", previously introduced to the group by Pissarro, was to have more of a future: Gauguin. He put nineteen paintings on view before going off to spend the summer in Pont-Aven. The exhibition apparently aroused the interest of a young Dutchman, a certain Vincent van Gogh, who had come to Paris to join his art dealer brother. In 1886, the story of Impressionism was over and that of Post-Impressionism was beginning. This general term groups together widely differing trends: the late works of Monet and Cézanne, Neo-Impressionism, the paintings of Gauguin and van Gogh, and the works of Toulouse-Lautrec and the Nabis... Henceforth, artists innovated alone, as is shown at the Orsay Museum in the way each painter is hung separately after 1880. They would all help to develop the main artistic trends of the beginning of the XXth century.

Paul Cézanne:
inventor of a new space

Of all the Impressionists, Cézanne was slighted the most. Public and critics alike rejected his work, even his friend Zola, who treated him as a failed genius by using him as the model for the hero of his book *L'Œuvre*. More innovative than his fellow painters, who immediately saw him as a master, he was late in winning recognition. The retrospective held in his honour at the Salon d'Automne in 1907 finally rendered him justice. His early paintings were characterised by his use of dark tones and heavy impasto. While he was with Pissarro, his colour range became lighter, but his Impressionist works remained more structured than those of his friends. Concerned with expressing space, without resorting to traditional perspective techniques, he elaborated a more geometrical style. The mobile and fleeting effects of nature did not interest him; on the contrary, he was trying to convey its permanence. From 1878 onwards, he stopped exhibiting with the Impressionists and settled in the South of France. A slow and solitary worker, his brief and oblique touches of colour create the space and volume of his canvases, in which the smallest detail is an integral part of the whole composition. Cézanne's style became progressively lyrical; the countryside surrounding Mount Sainte-Victoire inspired a series of paintings where the world is reduced to an inextricable network of vibrant touches of colour. In his own way, he had solved his contemporaries' overriding problem: how to express space through colour.

Paul Cézanne
(1839-1906),
L'Estaque,
circa 1878-1879,
oil on canvas,
59 × 73 cm.

The Mediterranean
light simplifies the
forms, reduces the
sea to a flat stretch of
intense blue in
contrast with the
foreground. In his
own compositions,
Caillebotte also used
empty spaces to set
off the strong
presence of a figure
or an architectural
feature.

Paul Cézanne
(1839-1906),
Pommes et oranges
(*Apples and
Oranges*)
circa 1895-1900,
oil on canvas,
74 × 93 cm.

A fruit bowl and a
jug viewed from the
front, a plate seen
from above!
However, the
composition retains
its overall
coherence: the
colour of the fruit is
echoed in the
background tapestry
and the motif on the
jug, as is the china in
the cloth's crisp
folds.

Neo-Impressionism
or the art of overcoming certainty

Pursuing radically divergent courses, the Neo-Impressionists also developed a veritable cult to colour. Like the Impressionists before them, they extolled colour and light, they depicted the modern world and sought to examine it objectively. At a time marked by a constant flow of scientific and technical innovation and a relentless stream of inventions, their scientific objectivity was well-placed. By setting off to observe nature "on the spot", and thus justifying their choice of aesthetics, the Impressionists had already adopted the attitude of their contemporaries, for whom science would eventually remove all uncertainty. But Seurat went even further and dreamt of a scientific art form, based on colour perception and optical treatises, where form and colour would be subject to laws of rational and immutable harmony. With rare indifference, he even said, "They see poetry in what I do... I apply my method and that's all."
He became the centre of a school of painting; Signac would faithfully pass on his Divisionist ideas and continue to find disciples after Seurat's premature death.

Gauguin
and the original primitive dream

Gauguin never missed an opportunity of deriding the Neo-Impressionists. Confronted with the materialism of an era fascinated by science and technical progress, he went back to his sources and set out in search of the primitive ideal. After the 1882 stock market crash, his mind was made up: at thirty-five years of age, he left the world of finance and a comfortable life behind, to devote all his time to painting. Up till then he had worked as an amateur with Pissarro. He went to Pont-Aven, where he hoped life would be cheaper, and invented Synthetism with the young Emile Bernard. Form and

Camille Pissarro (1830-1903), *Femme dans un clos* (*Woman in a Field*), 1887, oil on canvas, 54 × 65 cm.

Neo-Impressionist Pissarro: methodical fragmented brushwork and the obvious geometry of the trees' decrescent shadows.

Paul Signac (1863-1935), *La Bouée rouge* (*The Red Buoy*), 1895, oil on canvas, 81 × 65 cm.

The painter discovered Saint-Tropez in 1892. A less rigorous division of tones, warmer colours and larger dotted strokes may be noticed.

Theo van Rysselberghe (1862-1926), *L'Homme à la barre* (*Man at the Helm*), 1892, oil on canvas, 60.2 × 80.3 cm.

A friend Signac met during the organisation of the Les XX exhibitions in Brussels, Theo van Rysselberghe adopted Neo-Impressionisn in 1888.

Paul Gauguin
(1848-1903),
Le Cheval blanc
(*The White Horse*),
1898,
oil on canvas,
140 × 91.5 cm.

The Tahiti of
Gauguin's dreams:
an Eden untouched
by civilisation.
Cobalt blue water
with reflections of
orange, a red horse,
pink banks and a
rather green "white"
horse... Gauguin Pre-
Fauve.

Paul Gauguin

La Belle Angèle
(The Beautiful Angèle)
summer 1889
oil on canvas, 92 × 73 cm

Paul Gauguin (1848-1903) Gauguin started his working life as a stockbroker while painting as an amateur with Pissarro. He devoted himself entirely to painting from 1883 onwards. Leader of the Pont- Aven group of artists (*La Vision après le sermon – The Vision after the Sermon*, 1881), he was also admired by the Nabis. Other mediums he worked in were ceramics and sculpture. He first left for Tahiti in 1891 (*Sur la plage – On the Beach*, 1891) and settled there in 1895 (*Vairumati*, 1895).

Marie-Angélique Satre, hotel-keeper at Pont-Aven, had the reputation of being one of the most beautiful women in the village. When Gauguin asked her to pose for him, she accepted gracefully. But when the artist proudly came to give his model the painting, she refused it outright; indifferent to the composition's originality and the beauty of the colours, she thought she looked rather ugly. Degas, on the contrary, was captivated by this unusual portrait and eagerly bought it at the sale organised in 1891 to raise money for Gauguin's journey to the South Sea Islands. The beautiful Angèle is depicted in Breton costume, in a hieratic front view, her face revealing Gauguin's geometical treatment of volume. The lettered inscription enhances the portrait's solemnity. There is no semblance of truth in his treatment of space. Isolated in a circle that recalls the XIVth century Sienese mandorlas of the Virgin or Japanese crepons, beautiful Angèle stands out against an almost abstract background: watery tones with pink and white efflorescences at the top and a rich orange at the bottom. On the left is one of Gauguin's Peruvian-influenced ceramics. It seems like an exotic version of our Breton idol: the same frontality, simplified forms, hermetic face and the handles on the ceramic even form an aureole like a head-dress. Thus, while van Gogh searched for Japan in Arles, Gauguin found his primitive ideal in Brittany, where the villagers were still both deeply religious and often influenced by superstition and legend.

A doctor in attendance

Vincent van Gogh
(1853-1890),
Portrait of the Artist,
autumn 1887,
oil on canvas,
44.1 × 35.1 cm.

**Van Gogh in Paris.
The yellow self
portrait radiates
from the midnight-
blue
background.The air
shimmers under the
colour of the thick
brushstrokes that
herald the vibrant
skies of the Auvers-
sur-Oise period.**

colour were reduced to essentials, to add greater impact, and the paintings were composed of flat expanses of intense colour separated by strong outlines. Gauguin no longer restricted himself to merely depicting reality: he was ready to tackle symbolic and religious themes. A school built up around him with Sérusier as one of its most outstanding representatives. But from then on, Gauguin's life became one of perpetual wandering, from Pont-Aven to Tahiti, and from Tahiti to the Marquesas Islands. In his search for a truer civilisation, beset by solitude and destitution, his colours became progressively more intense, his forms cruder, mirroring the "primitive" he had dreamed of being.

Vincent van Gogh in search of the sun

When Gauguin and van Gogh's paths crossed in Arles, the impact was so strong that Vincent's fragile mental equilibrium was permanently impaired.

Three years earlier, on arriving in Paris to join his brother Theo, employed at the Goupil art gallery, van Gogh had discovered Impressionism and Neo-Impressionism. Within a few months, he had abandoned both the sombre tones of his "Dutch" palette and the social implications of his rural themes. He and his new friends celebrated modern Paris with its boulevards and cafés, the world of Montmartre and the suburbs, its dance halls and fortifications. A few months later, his fresh, bright colours developed a new, sometimes violent, intensity. He no longer used the fragmented brushstrokes of the Impressionists, nor the tiny dots of their successors, but expressed himself with increasingly assertive strokes. His brilliant colours, his brutally distorted human figures did not appeal to the public and left the critics indifferent: van Gogh could not sell his paintings. Like Gauguin, he looked for "somewhere else", somewhere

As soon as he arrived in Paris in 1848, medical student Paul Gachet became friends with a group of Realist painters whose Bohemian lifestyle he shared. He also painted himself in his spare time, and when he taught anatomy for artists in 1875, the young Seurat was one of his pupils. On buying his house at Auvers-sur-Oise in 1872, he immediately invited Cézanne and Guillaumin to stay. Dr. Gachet put his engraver's workshop at their disposal and began to collect his friends' works. Doctor to numerous artists, he treated Pissarro and Renoir's families with homeopathy. As he had studied mental illness and written a thesis on melancholia, Theo van Gogh came to him when looking for a doctor for his brother. Vincent arrived in Auvers in May, 1890, and he and the doctor immediately took to each other. Gachet, who signed his paintings "van Ryssel" ("From Lille" in Flemish), was, like van Gogh, a Northerner. The doctor's house in Auvers was always open to artists

**Norbert Goeneutte
(1854-1894),
Dr. Paul Gachet,
1891, oil on wood,
35 × 27 cm.**
One year separates this portrait from van Gogh's. A more Naturalist interpretation of the doctor.

**Vincent van Gogh
(1853-1890),
Dr. Paul Gachet,
June 1890, oil on canvas,
68 × 57 cm.**
The doctor's yellow and ochre face stands out against the deep blue, the red of the table and the complementary green of the plants, "What fascinates me is the modern portrait [...] I'm searching for it through colour."

and seemed like the community Vincent had dreamed of. Above all, Dr. Gachet encouraged his patient to paint, which van Gogh did relentlessly. In two months he finished over 75 canvases that, depending on his frame of mind, were either chaotic or magnificent. Paul and Marguerite Gachet's donations between 1949 and 1958 endowed the State with the doctor's collection: it includes the works painted by van Gogh at Auvers, as well as several Impressionist masterpieces by Pissarro, Cézanne and Guillaumin.

Vincent van Gogh

Vincent van Gogh (1853-1890) Former employee at the Goupil Gallery and attempted evangelist of the Borinage miners, Vincent van Gogh finally decided to become a painter. He enrolled at the Antwerp Academy in 1885; the following year he was in Paris and frequented Cormon's studio where he met the Impressionists. As a result he abandoned his sombre colours (*Le Restaurant de la sirène à Asnières – The "La Sirène" Restaurant in Asnières*, 1886). He left for Arles in February, 1888, and produced paintings with increasingly vivid colours like *L'Arlésienne – The Woman of Arles*. Gauguin joined him at the end of the year. Interned in 1889 at Saint-Rémy-de-Provence, he then went to Auvers-sur-Oise where he committed suicide in 1890.

La Chambre de van Gogh à Arles
(van Gogh's Room at Arles)
1889, oil on canvas, 57.5 × 74 cm

"I enjoyed myself enormously doing this bare interior..." This painting was one of van Gogh's favourites and exists in three versions. The one at Orsay is perhaps the most successful. The floor, pink in the first version, green in the second, is predominantly lilac with hints of pink, green and grey. The delicacy of these tones enhances the vibrant harmony in the flat areas of colour covering the rest of the canvas: deep blue, bright red, a few touches of green...not forgetting yellow, which, from ochre to lemon, illuminates this shadowless room. On arriving in Arles, van Gogh had hoped to create an artists' community where painters, freed of the material difficulties they struggled against in Paris, could work together in a spirit of friendly competition, inspired by the colours and light of the South. With this in mind, and overflowing with enthusiasm, Vincent began to get the "yellow house" ready in May, 1888, and moved in on September 18th. He started *the Tournesols* (*Sunflowers*) series and painted *La Chambre de van Gogh à Arles* (*van Gogh's Room at Arles*), while waiting for Gauguin to arrive on October 20th. This closed space is treated in the Japanese style, with a floor as the prevalent feature. The furniture and objects are arranged in such a way as to create a binary rhythym in the composition where each element has an echo: the bed and the table, the two chairs, the two drawings, the two portraits, the landscape and the mirror hung on either side of the window, the two doors, etc.

If Vincent spoke of a "bare interior", it is because there is no living presence in the room: the neatly-placed furniture along the walls leaves an unoccupied space in the middle of the canvas. The repeated vanishing lines traced on the floor emphasise this impression of emptiness and the heavy brushstrokes lead the eye quite naturally to the window at the back.

But the eye's vista stumbles on the greenish luminosity of the closed shutters. None of the doors and windows in the room give access to another space.
During his internment, Vincent would re-work this theme with little change in the composition that reminded him of his last peaceful moments, when he could still maintain a balance between extremes of tension: solitude and expectation, space and confinement, optimism and anguish...

The Caillebotte Affair

Degas, a singular artist

In 1894, a certain Gustave Caillebotte, painter and collector, bequeathed his paintings to the State, rather to its dismay. The collection included works by Degas, Monet, Cézanne, Pissarro and Sisley: the Caillebotte Affair exploded.

A friend of the Impressionists, Gustave Caillebotte had used his comfortable financial position to support them and to build up a collection of prestigious works that would engrave his name in history. Embarrassed by the legacy, the State equivocated before finally accepting. The paintings were housed in the Luxembourg Museum's new annexe inaugurated in 1897. They raised a general outcry: petitions were signed, polemics were launched and people even came to blows.

Gustave Caillebotte (1848-1894),
Les Raboteurs de parquet **(The Floor Scrapers),**
1875,
oil on canvas, 102 × 146.5 cm.
The modernity of a Haussmann-style apartment.
Caillebotte's Naturalism owes more to photography
than to Impressionism.

Edgar Degas (1834-1917),
Semiramis Overseeing the Construction of Babylon, 1861,
oil on canvas, 151 × 258 cm.
Degas the historical painter. Stagecraft already evident.

Edouard Manet (1832-1883),
The Balcony, 1868-1869, oil on canvas, 170 × 124 cm.
Group portrait including Berthe Morisot. A model of Realism
and modernity for Caillebotte who purchased it at the sale of
Manet's studio in 1884.

However the State had already made a ruthless selection: 27 canvases had been rejected, but Manet's *Le Balcon* (*The Balcony*), Monet's *Les Régates à Argenteuil* (*Sailing Boats at Argenteuil*) and Cézanne's *L'Estaque* entered the national collections. In homage to his brother, Martial Caillebotte, who together with Renoir undertook to see that the legacy was accepted, added two of Gustave's works, *Les Raboteurs de parquet* (*The Floor Scrapers*) and *Toits sous la neige* (*Roofs in the Snow*).

Gustave Caillebotte's discretion in leaving his own works out of the bequest is regretted today, since his talent was undeniable. His early paintings expressed a very personal Realism. A painter of Haussman's Paris, his urban views were subject to an insistent perspective and precise draughtsmanship. His unusual way of framing his compositions, and their neutral and contrasted colours are reminiscent of both photographs and Japanese prints: they have no equivalent in this period. At the end of the 1870s, he drew closer to Impressionism: boaters and canoes became part of his repertoire; his friends' bright colours and fragmented brushstrokes appeared in his works. Today, most of the canvases of the Caillebotte Collection, dispersed throughout the museum's collections, stand out as "key-works" in the history of Impressionism.

Like his friend Manet, Degas played a separate role in the history of Impressionism. A faithful member of the group exhibitions, which he hoped to make into a Realist Salon, he also applied himself to convey-

Edgar Degas, *Dans un café,*
also called *L'Absinthe,*
circa 1875-1876, oil on
canvas, 92 × 68 cm.
Two friends posed for him
work, butDegas gives the
illusion of an on the spot
scene.

ing movement in modern life: dancers, horses and women washing were his favourite themes. There were few landscapes among Degas' works: the open air was not good for his fragile eyesight, and he preferred indoor scenes, often artificially lit. As early as the 1860s, *La Famille Bellelli* (*The Bellelli Family*) could only be one of Degas' works. Despite his admiration for Ingres, the canvas marked a clear breaking away from classical art, without adhering to Courbet's Realist principles. Gifted with an insatiable curiosity, Degas experimented in various techniques: he mixed turpentine with oil colours to obtain a matt effect, practised the art of pastel and engraving , and reinvented the monotype. When he tackled sculpture, his idea was to capture the movement of a horse, the attitude of a dancer or a woman washing, which he would then transpose into his canvases. He also modelled his favourite subjects in wax: the Orsay Museum possesses a complete series cast after his death.

Edgar Degas,
Cheval cabré **(Rearing Horse),**
1888-1890,
bronze, 30 cm.

A raised sculpture capturing the attitude or movement to be used in painting.

lighter... and cheaper. He chose Arles, in the hope of founding a painters' "co-operative" where they would work together. Gauguin was the only one to accept the invitation, partly to please Theo, who was, after all, a dealer. Tension mounted quickly between the two artists, and on December 23rd 1888, van Gogh, in a fit of madness, cut off his ear. He was first interned at Saint-Remy, where he started to paint again, then sent to Auvers-sur-Oise, to be near Dr. Gachet. It was there that he worked feverishly to produce a striking series of paintings in which masterpieces like *Portrait of Doctor Gachet* and *L'Eglise d'Auvers-sur-Oise* (*The Church at Auvers-sur-Oise*) were interspersed with less successful attempts. In 1890, exhausted from work and solitude, he shot himself in the chest and ended his life.

Toulouse-Lautrec: nights in Montmartre

Ten years later, his friend from Cormon's studio, Henri de Toulouse-Lautrec also died, victim, in his own words, of a much slower "moral suicide." Descendant of a noble family from the South-West, the young Henri showed a precocious talent for drawing. He suffered from a rare bone disease that limited his growth. Encouraged by Degas, whose cynicism and talent he admired, he applied himself to expressing the movement of horses and dance and drew frequent portraits of his family, often stamped with an amused ferocity. He painted on cardboard that absorbed his mixture of pigment and turpentine and thus obtained matt coloured graphic effects. When he settled in the Montmartre district, his favourite haunts and sources of inspiration were the music-halls, circuses, cabarets and brothels that he drew without adopting a moral standpoint. The Moulin Rouge opened in 1889 and two years later, Toulouse-Lautrec, a regular client, created the poster that

Henri de Toulouse-Lautrec (1864-1901), *La Clownesse Cha-U-Kao* (*The Woman Clown, Cha-U-Kao*), 1895, oil on cardboard, 54 × 49 cm.

The woman clown's enveloping movement is as rounded as the dazzling sash of yellow gauze she is fitting to her midnight-blue bodice. The presence of a man is revealed in the mirror's reflection.

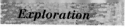

Japanism

was to make its name. His innovative talent as a poster designer and lithographer was phenomenal, and from 1894 onwards he moved in the *Revue blanche* circle. Although his vision was far removed from that of the Nabis, who had neither his Naturalist vigour, nor his Expressionist tones, Toulouse-Lautrec contributed to the success of their review.

The Nabis: end of the century prophets

The story of the Nabis (a Hebrew word meaning "prophets") began in 1888, when Sérusier showed Ranson, Bonnard and Denis, his friends from Julian's studio, together with Vuillard and Roussel, a mysterious panel he called *The Talisman*. It was a landscape in vivid colours, so Synthetic it was almost abstract, and painted in Pont-Aven following Gauguin's instructions. All these young artists were admirers of Cézanne, and even more influenced by Japanese art than their predecessors. The heavily marked outlines, the flat stretches of matt colour, the sinuous lines as well as the decorative use of fabric or wallpaper patterns, which distinguished their paintings, were all derived from their observation of Japanese prints. The Nabis exhibited together for the first time at the end of 1891, at the Galerie Le Barc de Boutteville, and included Bonnard's *Le Corsage à carreaux* (*The Check Blouse*) and Vuillard's *Au lit* (*In Bed*). The same year Vallotton joined the group, soon followed by Maillol. The Nabis produced panels and painted screens, displaying an interest in decorative art which broadened at the end of the century. Their allusive and Synthetic art was used in illustration, posters and lithography. Most of them collaborated with the *Revue Blanche*. The group broke up towards 1900, but they all went on individually to contribute to the development of XXth century art.

In 1853 Japan opened its doors to international trade. As a result, Westerners eagerly discovered Japanese objets d'art that were immediately exported and exhibited at World Fairs. Artists and art lovers collected Japanese ornaments, prints and crepons. The term "Japanism" was penned by art critic Philippe Burty and covered the whole range of Western interpretations of Japanese art: from the simple adaptation of Japanesque decorative motifs, the new version of XVIIIth century Chinese curios, to the analysis and integration of this art's principles.

Its refined aestheticism spread into the decoration of everyday objects and fabrics. The sinuous lines and plant motifs of Japanese prints and décors are expressed in the works of Art Nouveau. At the turn of the century, the most innovative architects and designers from Josef Hoffmann to Frank LLoyd Wright, were inspired by an art reduced to essentials, by its pure lines and décors. Painters also "went Japanese." Monet adorned the walls of his house with Japanese prints, for they echoed his own artistic choices: his love of nature, his strong, light colours. Manet borrowed another quite different aspect: it was the use of flat areas of colour and black that interested him. Gauguin found an alternative here–amid other exotic art forms–to the hackneyed rules of Western painting. The Pont-Aven group and the Nabis showed an even closer interest, especially Bonnard, the "Nabi japonard." In fact , from van Gogh to Redon and Toulouse-Lautrec, all the modern painters were influenced by Japanese art. Off-centre compositions became increasingly frequent in their works, as well as views from above, synthetic forms reduced to a few flat areas of colour and matt tones. But Japanese art also stimulated deeper analysis, especially in the field of graphic arts. Note Henri Rivière's remarkable woodcuts, *Trente-six vues de la Tour Eiffel* (*Thirty-six Views of the Eiffel Tower*), an undisguised homage to Hokusai, or Mary Cassatt's engravings directly inspired by the Japanese artist Utamaro's prints. To every artist his own "japonisme."

Tiffany and Company (from 1853 onwards), *Jug*, circa 1878, Partially hammer-wrought silver, copper and brass, 22 × 13.7 cm. This jug is purely Western in form while the Japanese influence is evident in its representation of nature, its use of fluid forms, and its hammer-wrought background inlaid with delicately coloured metals.

Paul Sérusier
(1864-1927),
The Talisman, 1888,
oil on wood,
27 × 21 cm.

Here, on Gauguin's
instructions,
landscape was
reduced to a few
areas of intense
colour. The work
that marked the
birth of the Nabi
movement.

Félix Vallotton
(1865-1925),
*Le Ballon ou Coin de
parc avec enfant
jouant au ballon*
(*The Ball*), 1899,
oil on cardboard,
48 × 61 cm.

A search for
simplification that
vividly contrasts
light colours and
radically flattens
form.

Edgar Degas

Petite Danseuse de quatorze ans
(Little Dancer of Fourteen)

Edgar Degas (1834-1917) After a brief attendance at the Ecole des Beaux-Arts and a long stay in Italy, Degas devoted his time to historical painting (*Semiramis*, 1861) and ambitious portraits (*The Bellelli Family*, 1858-1867) with the intention of presenting them at the Salon. From the early 1860s, he concentrated on subjects from modern life, moving closer to Manet and the Impressionists, with whom he exhibited until 1886. When he stopped working around 1907-1910, he was almost blind.

1879-1881, bronze, 95.2 cm

When Degas presented his *Little Dancer of Fourteen* to the public in 1881, it was an exploit. It was true that she had kept people waiting: the previous year, Degas, dissatisfied as usual, had decided not to display her, even though she was already in the exhibition catalogue and a showcase was ready for her. Despite her natural and spontaneous charm, the most Impressionist of sculptures had taken a long time to complete. Marie van Goethem, the model, was fourteen years of age in 1878: Degas had her pose nude and did several sketches of her, from which he prepared a small, first rough model in wax. He then undertook a second version, again in coloured wax, but this time dressed in a genuine tutu, ballet shoes and pink ribbon. To make her more real, he added doll's hair: the effect was striking. Huysmans saw in her "the only truly modern attempt at sculpture." The public was struck not so much by the technique–Degas was not alone in his use of wax–as by the adolescent's realistic morphology. Curiously, her large feet, short neck, low forehead and prominent jaw took away none of the work's overall grace, and helped to convey the model's childish banter. In 1903, *La Petite Danseuse*, also known as the *Grande Danseuse*, since it was Degas' biggest sculpture, was still to be found in the artist's studio, waiting to be cast in bronze. Not until 1921, four years after Degas' death, was this accomplished: the fragile effigy that was starting to crumble was saved.

Etienne Moreau-Nélaton, collector

Fellow student of Bergson and Jaurès at the Ecole Normale Supérieure, painter, engraver, ceramist, but above all prodigious collector and essayist on Manet, Delacroix, Jongkind, Corot and Daubigny, Etienne Moreau-Nélaton is one of the national museums' greatest donators.

If the idea of family tradition has a meaning, there is nothing surprising in the fact that Etienne became an important figure in the history of art. Grandfather Moreau, a friend of Delacroix and keen collector, accumulated more than 800 works at his house in Fère-en-Tardenois; they were essentially works related to the Romantic and Orientalist movements. Etienne's father, a collector in his turn, published two individual treatises on Delacroix and Decamps; he married Camille Nélaton, a talented painter and ceramist. Helped by family friends Rosa Bonheur and Henri Harpignies, Camille guided the first artistic attempts of her son Etienne, who decided to become a painter in 1882. In 1897, there was a catastrophe: he lost both his mother and his wife in a fire at a charity bazaar and went through a period of deep crisis. He then undertook to enlarge the collection he had inherited. An ardent admirer of contemporary painting, he chose works by Corot, Manet and the Impressionists. He immediately perceived the logical articulation leading from Delacroix's paintings to the Impressionist revolution, via Corot and the Barbizon group's discovery of landscape. It is thus as a XIXth century positivist, trusting in historical progress, that he built up his collection of master-

Edouard Manet (1832-1883), *Le Déjeuner sur l'herbe*, 1863, oil on canvas, 208 × 264.5 cm. Modern painting's manifesto-canvas...Impressionism's Mona Lisa, rendered homage countless times, both respected and defied.

Claude Monet (1840-1926), *Coquelicots – (Wild Poppies)*, 1873, oil on canvas, 50 × 65 cm. One of the most famous works of the Argenteuil period. The sky, the meadow undulating in the wind and the slight silhouettes that set the scale.

pieces. Corot's *Pont de Narni* (*Bridge at Narni*) and the *Cathédrale de Chartres* (*Chartres Cathedral*) are brilliant statements of Pre-Impressionism; Manet's *Le Déjeuner sur l'herbe* remains the XIXth century's symbol of modern painting; Fantin-Latour's *Hommage à Delacroix* (*Homage to Delacroix*) situates Manet, as early as 1864, in a historical perspective; Jongkind and Daubigny's works are direct forerunners of Impressionism; Monet's *La Route de Bas Bréau* (*The Road from Bas Bréau*) ensures, with the Barbizon school, the transition period, and heralds the Argenteuil works; a group of Sisley's paintings bears witness to his stylistic links with Corot...This collection is obviously a show of force.

Decided to apply all his weight, Etienne Moreau-Nélaton cleverly prepared his donation in 1906. When given 100 works, the Louvre, in order to acquire the Delacroix and Corot canvases, had to accept the Impressionists that until then had been exhibited in the Luxembourg Museum.

Today, the collection is divided between the Orsay Museum and the Louvre, which has kept the older works and the thirty-seven Corots. The first room of Orsay's "Galerie des Hauteurs" is arranged around Manet's *Le Déjeuner sur l'herbe*: dazzling Impressionist paintings mingle with the works of Carrière, a friend of the collector, Manet, Fantin-Latour and Puvis de Chavannes who had influenced Etienne Moreau-Nélaton's own output. In this way, the museum pays homage to the taste and perspicacity of his choice.

ITINERARY

'4

Exploration

■ Aspects of Naturalism
■ Rodin, sculptor of human passion
■ Pictorialism: the photo-tableau
■ A new glass age

Discoveries

■ Dalou's *Triumph of the Republic*
■ Cormon's *Cain*
■ Homer's *Summer Night*
■ Charpentier's *Dining-room*
■ Redon's *Portrait of Gauguin*

Encounter with

■ Proust, fin-de-siècle observer

Passage through the IIIrd Republic (1870-1914)

by Valérie Mettais

From 1870 to the turn of the century, political developments under the IIIrd Republic were reflected in academic art. Paintings and sculptures were essentially historical and allegorical glorifications to adorn public monuments and the Salon walls. Walls denied to canvases by innovative painters like the future Impressionists, who consequently decided to organise their own exhibitions. Painting thus started to evolve independently outside of official institutions. Naturalism retained certain Impressionist notions - the observation of nature and the choice of modern subjects - and became a recognised art form in the 1880s. The idealistic and spiritual inspiration of Symbolism existed parallel and in antithesis to this Realist exactitude. Ten years later, the stylistic revolution brought about by Art Nouveau, in its search for new forms and means of expression, threw the very relationship between art, decoration and architecture into upheaval. In reserving an extensive exhibition space for all these trends, some of which have seldom been viewed until now, the Orsay Museum provides the visitor with a panoramic vision of artistic life in the IIIrd Republic.

1870

Declaration of the Franco-Prussian War. Defeat at Sedan on 2 September and proclamation of the IIIrd Republic two days later.

1871

France lost the War. Violence under the Paris Commune.

1873

Mac Mahon became President of the Republic after Thiers' resignation.

1876

500,000 visitors at the Salon.

1878

Paris Exposition Universelle: construction of the first Palais du Trocadéro.

1879

Mac Mahon was succeeded by Jules Grévy as President of the Republic. Constitution of the French Labour party. *La Marseillaise* became the national anthem.

1880

Amnesty of the Paris Communards; 14 July declared a national holiday. 3,000 canvases exhibited at the Salon. Rodin began *La Porte de l'Enfer* (*The Gate of Hell*).

1881

Jules Ferry established free, compulsory, secular education under a law bearing his name.

1885

Sadi Carnot replaced Jules Grévy.

1886

Publication of Jean Moréas' *Manifeste symboliste*. Eighth and last Impressionist Exhibition.

1889

Inauguration of the Eiffel Tower during the Paris Exposition Universelle.

1894

Assassination of Sadi Carnot. Beginning of the Dreyfus Affair.

1895

Félix Faure elected President of the Republic. First Paris film projection by the Lumière brothers. Paris art dealer Siegfried Bing opened his gallery "Art Nouveau" in the rue de Provence.

1898

Publication of Zola's *J'accuse* dans *l'Aurore* in defence of Dreyfus who was pardoned in 1899 and reinstated in 1906. Death of Puvis de Chavannes and Gustave Moreau.

1899

Guimard designed the cast-iron entrances to the Parisian underground stations.

1900

Construction of the Grand and Petit Palais, the Alexander III Bridge and the underground railway for the Paris Exposition Universelle. Inauguration of Orsay Station, built by Victor Laloux.

1905

Separation of the Church and the State. Russian Revolution and the battleship *Potemkine* mutiny.

1913

Publication of Marcel Proust's *Du côté de chez Swann*, first volume of *A la recherche du temps perdu*.

1914

Assassination of Jaurès. Start of the First World War.

After twenty years of Empire, the young IIIrd Republic, proclaimed on 4 September 1870, had to establish its respectability, legitimise its values and reinforce its authority. In addition it had to recover from the defeat inflicted at Sedan by the Prussians, which led to the loss of Alsace-Lorraine, and to forget the blood spilt during and after the Paris Commune. The Republic committed itself to instruction and the spreading of knowledge: images were therefore needed.

Historical painting and heroic sculpture

Official commissions for historical paintings, allegorical décors and monumental sculptures rained and adorned new buildings erected to the glory of the Republic and the Salons dedicated to the fine arts. "Following an old convention, established by long usage, we attach an idea of moral purpose to decorating the walls of public edifices. We bestow upon them the role of consecration, commemoration or noble education," declared Léonce Bénédite, member of the French Institute. Numerous examples may be found in the two rooms at the Orsay Museum dedicated to arts and decoration during the IIIrd Republic.

Jules Dalou

Le Triomphe de la République
(The Triumph of the Republic)
1879-1899
Place de la Nation, Paris, bronze, 12 × 6.5 × 12 m

Jules Dalou
(1838-1902).
A sculptor trained at
the Ecole des Beaux-
Arts, Dalou
collaborated with
Carpeaux on the
decoration of private
mansions in Paris. A
radical Republican,
he was forced into
exile after the
Commune. He
returned to Paris in
1879 after the
Communards were
amnestied, and
received several
commissions. His
small sculptures and
his public
monuments with
their everyday life
themes of peasants
and workers were
realistically treated
and exalted the
values
of the IIIrd Republic.

**Preparatory works
in museum care:**
The Republic,
terracotta,
33 × 14 cm.
The Republic,
plaster, 57 × 27 cm.
The Blacksmith,
plaster, reduced
scale model 1:6,
67 × 37 cm.

The IIIrd Republic multiplied its
commissions for public monuments
with a political theme as a means of
imposing its power. Thus, in 1879,
the Paris municipal authorities held
a competition for a statue to
decorate the entrance to the
Faubourg du Temple. Seventy-nine
projects for statues representing
the Republic were submitted.
Among them was that of Dalou, in
exile in London since the fall of the
Commune. His plaster model was
much admired, but it was Léopold
Morice's more traditional and

solemn monument that was chosen
and inaugurated on 14 July 1883, in
the Place de la République.
Naturalist inclined Dalou had
introduced realistic figures in his
project: beside the triumphant
Republic in her revolutionary
Phrygian cap, standing upright on a
chariot pulled by two lions, and
accompanied by the allegorical
figures of Liberty, Plenty, Justice
and Peace, is thus found Labour, a
blacksmith wearing clogs, rough
trousers and apron, and carrying a
hammer on his shoulder. In this
allegorical composition it is the
Republican hero - the labourer -
who triumphs. Bought by the Paris
municipal authorities, Dalou's
model would not be cast in bronze
until twenty years later. *The
Triumph of the Republic* was finally
inaugurated in the Place de la
Nation in 1899: its thirty-eight-ton
casting was the largest ever
undertaken in the XIXth century.

Patriotism was nurtured by historical painting; Ernest Meissonier, Alphonse de Neuville, Edouard Detaille and Georges Clairin, with *L'Incendie des Tuileries* (*The Burning of the Tuileries*), depicted the bloody episodes of that "terrible year" between 1870 and 1871: "This century is before the Court and I am its witness," proclaimed Victor Hugo on his return from exile. Whether document, testimony, allegory or political glorification, painting exalted the IIIrd Republic's national sentiment. It was also devoted to recalling the past, from Prehistory with Cormon's *Cain* in 1880, through the Middle Ages with Jean-Paul Laurens' *The Excommunication of Robert the Pious* in 1875, to the representation of great historical figures, like Joan of Arc and Charlemagne, or statesmen and scientists from Gambetta to Pasteur. In their attention to detail and their precise technique, scenes from history sought authenticity or truth, an aspiration also striven after by photography. Since the invention of the daguerreotype in 1839, both documentary and artistic photography had rivalled painting and become an art in its own right.

Monumental sculpture complied with the same educational and social requirements. It reached its apex and was erected on every square glorifying national heroes and decorating buildings.

Antonin Mercié received the gold medal at the 1874 Salon for his *Gloria Victis*, a vibrant figure calling for the nation's restoration; for the 1878 Exposition Universelle, Auguste Clesinger set up an antique effigy of the Republic, while Bartholdi's *Statue of Liberty* confirmed Franco-American friendship. Historical or allegorical representation of history also inspired Alexandre Falguière, Paul Cabet and Paul Dubois' *Alsace and Lorraine* in 1899. An epic, baroque note may be found in Emmanuel Frémiet's great *Saint Michael* of 1896.

Paul Cabet
(1815-1876),
*Eighteen Hundred
and Seventy-one,*
1872-1877, marble,
125 × 66 cm.

An allegorical
expression of the
drama of the 1871
capitulation, the loss
of Alsace-Lorraine
and the Commune
uprising.

Gustave Doré
(1832-1883),
The Enigma, 1871,
oil on canvas,
130 × 195 cm.

"The terrible year",
that of the war with
Prussia and the Paris
Commune, inspired
painters to execute
commemorative and
allegorical
compositions: a
winged figure
questions the Sphinx
on a corpse-strewn
battlefield against a
background of Paris
in ruins.

Fernand-Anne Piestre, known as Cormon

Caïn

1880
oil on canvas,
384 × 700 cm

Fernand-Anne Piestre, known as Cormon (1845-1924) Member of the Institute and Salon medal winner, Cormon was one of the IIIrd Republic's great official painter-decorators. His monumental compositions, Realist in tone and with broad, thick brushwork, were inspired by biblical, mythological and prehistoric themes, such as *Cain* in 1880 and *L'Age de pierre* (*The Stone Age*) in 1884. It was in his teaching studio at the Ecole des Beaux-Arts that Emile Bernard, Toulouse-Lautrec and Van Gogh would meet.

"When with his children clothed in animal skins,
Dishevelled, ashen amid storms,
Caïn fled before Jehovah."
This vast composition with "life-size" figures illustrated the lines of Victor Hugo, taken from *La Conscience* of 1859, in *La Légende des Siècles*. Cormon depicted the first murderer of all time: Cain, who, out of jealousy, killed his brother Abel and had to flee to escape the curse of God.
In the middle of the desert, under an immense sky, the old man, armed with a bone axe, laboriously leads his tribe; his four sons transport a slumbering woman and children on a wooden stretcher covered in blood-stained skins. Two men accompany them, one with a stake over his shoulder and the hunted game slung bandoleer-like across his chest, the other carries a young girl in his arms; hunters and dogs bring up the rear. A relentless sky hangs heavily over the deserted landscape; the horizon line crosses the canvas in a pronounced diagonal. The procession's huge shadows extend forward: truth and divine vengeance seem to pursue the guilty. The painting's rough treatment, the broad brushstrokes on the irregular surface, and the earthy, ochre tones heighten The scene's tragic aspect.
At the 1880 Salon, Cormon illustrated one of his specialities: painting inspired from prehistory, which at that time aroused a great deal of interest. *Cain*, an ambitious archeological and anthropological reconstitution of the life of our ancestors, was carefully prepared by Cormon, who painted each figure from a living model, whom he had pose in his studio. This search for anatomical exactitude earned him the nickname "Father Kneecap" among his students at the Ecole des Beaux-Arts!

Cain was the major event at the 1880 Salon: bought by the State for ten thousand francs, it came close to winning the medal of honour that went to Aimé Morot's *Good Samaritan*, and earned its painter the rank of Officer of the Legion of Honour. The Naturalist treatment of this grandiloquent epic, did not fail to attract public attention, praise, fury and sarcasm. Some remained

hesitant before this audacious, archeological reconstitution, "This painting is both very good and very ugly [...]. This young painter knows very well that his characters are anterior to the Stone Age, that they preceded combs and soap by an infinite number of centuries, and that they are very little different from [...] the great apes of Equatorial Africa," wrote novelist and critic Edmond About. Others like Georges Lafenestre, Fine-Arts Academy inspector, overflowed with admiration in front of such an "abundance of invention, energy of expression, breadth of style." But the defenders of modern art were merciless: Emile Zola totally ignored the work, while Joris-Karl Huysmans dedicated a single, murderous sentence, "May I point out among other things the good old dotard featured at the front of the very mediocre *Cain*." It was the symbol of official Naturalism under the IIIrd Republic: painting with historical pretensions henceforth borrowed Courbet and Daubigny's effects of light and thick brushwork, once excluded from the Salons.

The institutions and academic glory

The Ecole des Beaux-Arts, the Institute and the Salon were the three cultural pillars of the IIIrd Republic: the former for its academic teaching based on the study of Antiquity and the Renaissance, the Institute for its regulation of artistic life, and the increasingly crowded Salons for exhibition and reception of State purchases and commissions. The 1876 Salon attracted over five hundred thousand visitors; more than three thousand canvases were displayed at the one in 1880. Glory and medals went to either allegorical, religious or historical painting that was still judged superior and so occupied the place of honour in the hierarchy of genres. It was also a pretext for depicting the female nudes so highly appreciated by the public and collectors: thus William Bouguereau's *La Naissance de Vénus* (*The Birth of Venus*) in 1879 exposed her smooth body amid more conventional cherubims. By the end of the century, academic painting had exhausted itself through its virtuosity in a technique inspired by Raphaël and Ingres, retaining only the sensual or licentious aspects of mythological themes. "Wax, glass, icing sugar, I don't know, but I feel that looking at this painting for a long time would make one nauseous," said ironically defender of Realism critic Jules Castagnary about this same Bouguereau, one of the most renowned painters: in 1900 a master canvas cost one hundred thousand francs while a miner's salary averaged one thousand francs. Sculpture inspired from Antiquity or religion was stamped with this same eroticism, as may be seen in Alexandre Schoenewerk's *La Jeune Tarentine* (*Young Woman from Tarente*), in 1871, Eugène Delaplanche's *Eve avant le péché* (*Eve Before Sin*), in 1891, and Jean-Léon Gérôme's *Tanagra*, in 1890.
The portrait vogue that flourished at the Salons continued, and the society portrait enjoyed an extraordinary success. Artists, dandies and actresses, like Sarah Bernhardt or

Léon Bonnat
(1833-1922),
Madame Pasca, 1874,
oil on canvas,
222 × 132 cm.

The Salons of the IIIrd Republic were filled with academic portraits: full-length studies of actresses, society personalities, businessmen and politicians.

Eugène Carrière
(1849-1906),
Paul Verlaine, 1890,
oil on canvas,
61 × 51 cm.

In a monochrome of
ochres and browns,
Carrière portrayed
the poet who
embodied the
Symbolist
generation.

Lucien Lévy-
Dhurmer
(1865-1953),
*The Woman with the
Medal* or *Mystery,*
1896,
pastel, 34 × 54 cm.

Using his favourite
technique of pastel,
Lévy-Dhurmer
conveyed in refined
tones figures imbued
with mystery and
sensuality.

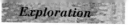

Aspects of Naturalism

Count Robert de Montesquiou, portrayed by Léon Bonnat, Carolus-Duran, Giovanni Boldini and Jacques-Emile Blanche, revealed the elegance, fashions, luxury and eccentricities of the "Belle Epoque" in this cosmopolitan Paris.

Naturalism and the choice of modern subjects

Besides historical or mythological scenes and society portraits, the Salon gradually began to accept pictures drawn from working-class life. Thirty years previously, Gustave Courbet, who created a scandal with his immense composition *Un enterrement à Ornans* (*A Burial at Ornans*), had already embarked on the Realist crusade. Under the IIIrd Republic, Naturalist painting succeeded Realism and extended its teachings through its choice of modern subjects, its frank technique and large-scale treatment of peasants and working men. In 1882, five years after his death, the retrospective of Courbet's works at the Ecole des Beaux-Arts was a clear sign of this evolution.

In literature with Emile Zola, in painting and then in sculpture, Naturalism extolled precise observation of nature, scenes from working-class life, and henceforth adopted a social dimension. Jules Bastien-Lepage was its herald: *Les Foins* (*Haymaking*), exhibited in 1877, demonstrated its attention to rural life and borrowed its luminous, light tones and open-air freshness from the Impressionists. Bastien-Lepage, whom Zola called a "kind of deserter from the Ecole des Beaux-Arts coming back to a sincere study of nature," embodied the passage from Realism, rejected by the Salons, to the officially recognised and triumphant Naturalism of the 1880s. This social vein may also be seen in the works of Alfred Roll, Jean-Charles Cazin or Cormon's *Forge* of 1894. Meanwhile, the sombre and tragic canvases of Charles Cottet and Lucien Simon, members of the "Black Group", an

Contemporary with the IIIrd Republic's social policies, work regulation laws and the creation of trade unions, was the success of Naturalism that became an official art-form in the 1880s. Emile Zola, author of *L'Assommoir* and *Germinal*, undertook a study of the working world, while painters and sculptors devoted themselves to depicting everyday, rural and working-class scenes. Whether through allegorical studies of the worker, denunciation of

Marie Bashkirtseff 1860-1884),
A Meeting, 1884,
oil on canvas, 193 × 177 cm.
Student of Jules-Bastien-Lepage, Marie Bashkirseff retained his taste for modern subjects, broad brushstrokes and light palette, characteristic of Naturalism in the 1880s.

misery or simple picturesque representation, Naturalism spread across Europe.

In France, Jules Bastien-Lepage, Jean-Charles Cazin with *La Journée Faite* (*The Day Over*) of 1888, and Alfred Roll concentrated on rural life; sculptor Jules Dalou endowed his blacksmith and peasant figures with magnitude and dignity.

In Belgium, painter and sculptor Constantin Meunier dedicated himself to depicting miners and workmen. *Le Débardeur*

du port d'Anvers (*The Stevedore from Antwerp Harbour*) of 1890 or *The Puddlers* of 1893 were symbols of this social realism that replaced the historico-mythological heroes by the modern, turn-of-the-century, working man. Likewise, Bernhardt Hoetger evoked the *Human Machine* in his bas-relief of 1902. Max Liebermann in Germany, Peder Severin Kroyer in Denmark, Anders Zorn in Sweden, Georges-Hendrik Breitner and his *Horses Pulling Logs in Amster-*

dam of 1898, Sorolla y Bastida and *Hauling up the Boat* of 1895 in Spain, up to Russian artists like Marie Bashkirtseff, Bastien-Lepage's pupil in Paris, were other representatives of this movement. In 1894, the American Lionel Walden painted a large composition, *Cardiff Docks*.

Due to its extensive growth throughout Europe, Naturalism became one of the strongest official trends of the turn of the century.

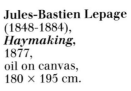

Jules-Bastien Lepage
(1848-1884),
Haymaking,
1877,
oil on canvas,
180 × 195 cm.

This painting is the
symbol of
Naturalism in its
modern rural theme,
its light palette and
its broad brushwork
inherited from the
Impressionists.

Léon Lhermitte
(1844-1925),
Harvesters' Pay,
1882,
oil on canvas,
215 × 272 cm.

Leader of officially
accepted Naturalism,
Léon Lhermitte
combined
observation of rural
life with exaltation
of social values:
rustic dignity,
motherhood, respect.

Winslow Homer

Summer Night
1890,
oil on canvas, 76 × 102 cm

Painter, illustrator and water-colourist, Homer was a symbol, during his own lifetime, of the American artist, a witness of everyday life who exalted essential human values.
He began his career as an artist-reporter in the American Civil War and went on to realistically depict the lives of soldiers and country people. After a stay in Paris, he temporarily adopted the Impressionist palette. In the Maine village where he settled, Homer brought a strange poetic sense to his paintings of sailors' existence.

Beside the ocean, two women are dancing; one of them is wearing a white dress. The couple is bathed in moonlight and probably in the lamplight from a nearby house. To their right the dark outlines of a group are discernible. The froth on the waves stands out against the blue water and horizon.
Winslow Homer, an American painter known for his pictures of contemporary life, left New York in 1882 to settle permanently on the Maine coast, in a small fishing village north of Boston called Prout's Neck. From then on, he devoted himself to landscapes, spending whole days watching the effects and changes of atmosphere and light; he even built a hut in which to shelter from storms. He also portrayed scenes from the lives of sailors, and it was in this village that he painted *Summer Night*.
The theme of this canvas seems to have been inspired by the reality of fishermen's everyday existence, observed from the ocean shore. Yet a strange feeling, a mixture of melancholy and sensual tension, emanates from the work. Time seems to stand still as the two women dance. The figures sitting with their backs to them are almost spectral silhouettes that blend into the shadows on the beach. The extremely long horizon line stretches out of sight.
Winslow Homer used the chiaroscuro effect to play on contrast and to set off forms against the sombre sky and turquoise sea while diagonal, white brushstrokes enhance the frothy waves. This totally poetic evocation of a nocturnal seascape, and the extended two women dancing theme, links Winslow Homer's art to that of European Symbolists Fernand Khnopff or Edvard Munch. It is interesting to compare the American's *Summer Night* with the

Norwegian's *Summer Night at Aasgaardstrand* of 1904; the same subject, the same familiar location, a small fishing village, inspired

them both: the former suggested poetry and mystery through Realism and observation; the latter's violent expression in its accentuated diagonals and acidic colours was close to Expressionism. Homer's *Summer Night*, acquired by the State at the 1900 Exposition Universelle for the Luxembourg Museum, introduces the visitor to XIXth century American painting, still rare in French collections.

artists' community in Brittany, depicted the lives of seafarers and religious themes. Naturalism rapidly became a European movement. The Orsay Museum exhibits several representatives: the Dutchman Georg Hendrik Breitner, the Dane Peter Severin Kroyer, the Belgian Léon Frédéric,

the German Max Libermann and the Spaniard Sorolla y Bastida.

Sculptors around 1880 were subject to the same Naturalist principles. The warriors, mythological heroes and operetta shepherds that populated the Salons of the Second Empire were replaced by real figures, true social allegories of working people and Republican values. From 1879-1889 Jules Dalou created his monumental work, *Le Triomphe de la République* (*The Triumph of the Republic*), that was to sit in state over the Place de la Nation; *Le Forgeur* (*The Blacksmith*) was one of its elements. His more intimist sculptures of peasant women, seamstresses and women washing reveal his passion for everyday life, with neither historical pretext nor affectation. The *Grand Paysan* (*The Peasant*) of 1898-1900, a massive and powerful bronze, bore witness to his unfinished project *Monument au travail* (*Monument to Labour*). This dream of erecting a monument to the glory of the working man was shared by Constantin Meunier, whose Naturalist bas-reliefs were inspired by the lives of workers, dockers and miners.

Symbolism and the importance of the imagination

Parallel to Naturalism, an artistic, intellectual, philosophical, literary and musical movement known as Symbolism broke out all over Europe. In antithesis to an art form too close to reality, painters, sculptors and poets proposed one of mystical, idealistic and spiritual inspiration. They explored the world of dreams and fantasy and vindicated the importance of imagination: real life was to be replaced by the inner life, observation was to give way to subjective vision. The Impressionists were even considered "low-ceiling" by Odilon Redon: "True parasites clinging to the object, they cultivated art on a purely visual level, somehow excluding all that goes beyond and that could include, in humble attempts, even in black, the light of spirituality."

As early as 1848, the English Pre-Raphaelites' rejection of reality was already evident through their choice of esoteric subjects and their technique inspired by that of the Italian Primitives, as may be seen in Edward

Odilon Redon

Portrait of Gauguin
1903-1905
oil on canvas, 66 × 54 cm

Odilon Redon
(1840-1916).
An independent
artist at the end of
the century, after his
engraver's
apprenticeship with
Rodolphe Bresdin,
Redon developed a
black Romanticism,
illustrated in his
charcoal drawings
and lithographs
peopled with
oneiric, monstrous
and terrifying
figures. It was his
Black period.
From 1895-1900
colour and
light invade his
paintings (*Les Yeux
Clos - Eyes Closed*,
1890) and his
flower-strewn
pastels inspired
from mythological
themes. One of
Gauguin's friends,
and admired by the
Nabis, Huysmans
and Mallarmé,
Redon was a master
for the new
Symbolist
generation.

Despite its luxuriant colours, this portrait, one painter's homage to another, was painted in mourning and was the effigy of a deceased man. Paul Gauguin died on 8 May 1903, in the hut he had humorously and provocatively named his *Maison du jouir* (*House of Pleasure*), on the island of Hiva Oa. Fleeing civilisation in his search for an untouched world and another light, Gauguin had chosen one of the Marquesas Islands as his last place of residence. Shaken by this death, Odilon Redon painted two portraits of his friend from memory: one pastel, *Homage to Gauguin*, and this painting, then called *Le Profil Noir, Gauguin* (*Black Profile, Gauguin*). Redon, who took part in the last and eighth Impressionist Exhibition in 1886 together with Gauguin, admired the latter's courageous departure and defended, in the newspaper *Le Mercure de France*, the works his friend had presented in Paris: "What I like in him is the sumptuous and princely ceramist: he has created new forms here. I can compare them to flowers from a primary region, in which each flower would be the sample for a species, leaving future artists to provide affiliated varieties." And, in this painting, radiantly bright flowers encircle the model's face, described by critic Charles Morice as "bony and heavy with a narrow forehead and a nose, not bent, not hooked, but as if broken." In this sombre profile plunged in flowers, Redon sought a poetic, mysterious and magical evocation of the artist; he established a dialogue between Gauguin's face and the surrounding colours and forms, and fused reality with an unknown universe. More than just a portrait, this work is a homage, such as Gauguin imagined it. In a letter of his, dated September 1890, he effectively

wrote, "I remember one of Wagner's sentences that explains what I think: I believe that disciples of great art will be glorified and that, wrapped in a heavenly fabric of lightbeams, perfumes and melodious chords, they will return to lose themselves for eternity in the bosom of the divine source of all harmony." So, my dear Redon, we shall meet again."
Redon thus developed a new kind of portrait that was symbolist in conception and departed from the rules of the academic or society portrait: it escaped description and rejected end- of-the-XIXth century, Naturalist exactitude. Gauguin, with his *La Belle Angèle* of 1889, had also produced a strange portrait, placing a Breton peasant woman within a circle beside a small ceramic idol and flowering branches.
The painter and his model thus meet: they both participated in the development of Symbolism, the aim of which was to transcribe "correspondences" between the realms of dream and reality, as Baudelaire had already sought in his poetry; Gauguin, through his Synthetic vision, his flat areas of colour, his need for exoticism; Redon through his desire to express the inexpressible, and, as Maurice Denis remarked, to surrender the individual, in his paintings, charcoal drawings and pastels "to the whims of the unconscious."

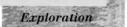

Pictorialism:

the photo-tableau

Burne-Jones' *The Wheel of Fortune* of 1883. Exhibited on the ground floor of the museum, in the first part of the visit, Pierre Puvis de Chavannes' allegorical compositions, from *Jeunes Filles au bord de la mer* (*Young Women at the Seaside*) of 1879 to *Rêve* (*Dream*) of 1883, opened the way to Symbolism: hieratic, timeless figures, a poetic evocation in softly-rounded forms and pale colours. Similarly, Gustave Moreau's phantasmagoria and preciosity were in complete harmony with these fin-de-siècle aesthetics. His canvases, with their biblical and mythological themes, were admired by the hero in *A Rebours*, Joris-Karl Huysmans' 1884 Symbolist novel.

The Orsay Museum has an excellent collection of Odilon Redon's drawings, lithographs and paintings thanks to his son Arï's donation. From charcoal drawings to the strange luminosity of his pastels, his interior décors, portraits or flower bouquets, Redon developed an essentially mysterious art open to immateriality, phantasma and the world of the unconscious, as depicted in *Les Yeux Clos* (*Eyes Closed*) of 1890. It was contemporary with Sigmund Freud's research: *The Interpretation of Dreams* dates from 1899.

In Eugène Carrière's grey and brown monochromes his portraits and scenes of motherhood were blurred and drowned in shadow; he thus created scarcely discernible, scarcely real, evanescent figures.

The Symbolist exhibitions bore witness to the thriving movement in France and other European countries, such as the Salon dedicated to the Rosicrucians, an order founded in 1890 by Sâr Péladan, or, in Brussels the group known as Les XX, formed in 1883 and replaced ten years later by La Libre Esthétique. Belgian Symbolism is represented at the Orsay Museum by Fernand Khnopff's melancholic portrait of *Marie Monnom* and by James Ensor's anguished figure *La Dame en détresse* (*The Lady in Distress*).

The Swiss painter Arnold Böcklin peopled his vast, half-real, half-imaginary land-

The end of the 1870s saw the simplification of photographic technique, tested and developed since the daguerreotype's invention in 1839: the new instantaneous and portable cameras put photography within everyone's reach. Enthusiasts who formed associations and clubs objected to the medium's purely mechanical or documentary value and asserted its claim to artistic status and originality. The photographer's eye

techniques, gum-bichromate, heavy inks, heliogravure, and platinum prints gave their work an air of charcoal drawings or engravings. Pictorialism rapidly developed into an international movement. Associations sprang up in Paris, with the Photo Club founded in 1894 that brought together Robert Demachy, Constant Puyo and Maurice Bucquet, in Hamburg, Brussels, London and Vienna. Two trends became apparent: one of

Edward Steichen (1879-1973),
Rodin, 1903, photogravure, 21 × 16 cm.
Published in the New York review *Camera Work.*
In a strident chiaroscuro, Rodin's silhouette stands out against the background statue of Victor Hugo shaded in white.

played a major role in Pictorialism, originally a British movement. It was inspired by its forerunner Peter Henry Emerson, together with Oscar Rejlander and Julia Margaret Cameron.

The Pictorialists advocated, both in composition and their printing mediums, a pictural rendering close to that of the Impressionists. They specialised in blurred effects, misty atmosphere and photographs taken against the light. Their

more pictural inspiration, the other more photographic, represented by the Austrian Heinrich Kühn, Englishman Frederick Evans and Americans Clarence Hudson White and Adolf de Meyer. Alfred Stieglitz, cofounder with Edward Steichen in 1902 of the New York Photo Secession group, developed a modernist approach that exploited the resources of photographic vocabulary and opened the way to the XXth century.

Pierre Puvis de Chavannes (1824-1898), *The Poor Fisherman*, 1881, oil on canvas, 155 × 192 cm.

The fisherman's meditative solemnity, the spareness of composition and soft tones fascinated Symbolist painters Odilon Redon and Eugène Carrière, and poets Stéphane Mallarmé, Joris-Karl Huysmans and Camille Mauclair.

Henri Rivière (1864-1951), *A Couple Entering a Building,* 1885-1895, matte silver print, 12 × 9 cm.

End of the century photography sought to recapture the intimacy, immediacy and spontaneity of an everyday Parisian scene.

Julia Margaret Cameron (1815-1879), *Portrait of Julia Duckworth, Virginia Woolf's mother,* circa 1866, albumen print from collodion glass negative, 22 × 16 cm.

Textural and blurred effects give this portrait a strange allure that is almost Symbolist in nature.

scapes with mythological creatures. "One is stupefied by this coherence in the dream, by this infatuation with weird fantasy, by this utter naturalness in the supernatural," wrote poet Jules Laforgue on Böcklin's work. In Italy, with Pelizza da Volpedo, or in the United States with Winslow Homer, Symbolist aesthetics fulfilled Mallarmé's wishes: "The gradual evocation of an object to reveal a mood, or, inversely, the choice of an object that conveys a mood, through a series of decipherments."

In the field of sculpture, Auguste Rodin's personality dominated the end of the century. *L'Age d'Airan* (*The Bronze Age*) in 1877 was followed by several monumental sculptures, such as *La Porte de l'Enfer* (*The Gate of Hell*), begun in 1880, and society or heroic portraits. Sculptor of fragments and works left unfinished, Rodin was a Realist in his sense of modelling, Symbolist in his inspiration and Expressionist in his bold distortion: his statue of *Balzac* shocked the 1898 Salon public. A large part of the upper level terrace in the Orsay Museum, at the back of the nave, is devoted to he who both embodied and went beyond the spirit of the century: the early XXth century sculptors either followed in Rodin's footsteps or rebelled against him: Emile-Antoine Bourdelle, Aristide Maillol, Medardo Rosso, Joseph Besnard, right up to Constantin Brancusi.

Art Nouveau: the invention of a decorative vocabulary

Alongside and aesthetically close to the Symbolist movement, Art Nouveau was a short-lived but powerful trend that appeared in the 1890s, highly innovative and internationally widespread from London to Paris and from Brussels to Barcelona. Inspired by plant life, it reinvented architectural forms and threw decorative vocabulary into upheaval. It was based on then revolutionary principles and abolished the distinction between "major arts" (painting and sculpture) and "minor arts" (furniture design, stained-glass windows, ceramics, glasswork and goldsmithery). Collaboration between artists and craftsmen (architects,

Louis-Ernest Barrias (1841-1905), *Nature Unveiling Herself to Science*, 1899, polychrome marble, onyx, lapis lazuli and malachite, 200 × 85 cm.

When academic art also serves as a pretext for eroticism. Nature unveils the charms of her anatomy, while the sculptor reveals his virtuosity in the combination of multicoloured marble and stones.

sculptors, carpenters, cabinet-makers, ironsmiths), the search for unity of form and its decoration, the use of curved lines and the respect for material – wood, cast-iron, wrought-iron, ceramics – were Art Nouveau's essential principles. It rejected eclecticism's pastiches and overladen style that had dominated decorative arts and the 1878 and 1889 Expositions Universelles. Art Nouveau's defenders extolled the radically

Auguste Rodin (1840-1917), *The Walking Man*, 1905, bronze, 213 × 161 × 72 cm.

Rodin, sculptor of fragments and reassembly: in this extraordinarily powerful headless, armless man, he reunites a torso and the legs of *St. John the Baptist*, created in 1877-1878.

Rodin, sculptor
of human passion

Auguste Rodin
Fugit Amor, 1880-1882, bronze, 30.8 × 46 × 33.5 cm.
In this element from *The Gate of Hell*, representing the
damned lovers Paolo and Francesca in Dante's *Inferno*, Rodin
contrasts rough-hewn marble with the fluidity of the bodies'
modelling.

He has been, in turn, the torture and exaltation of Delight, the pain of Life, and the terror of Death with [The Gate of] Hell; the voice of History with the Burghers of Calais; the clash of the elements with Victor Hugo; manifold Humanity with Balzac," wrote poet Rainer Maria Rilke on the subject of Rodin. The figure that dominated XIXth century sculpture, exemplary all-round artist, impassioned sculptor but also draughtsman and lithographer, Rodin tackled all subjects, drew inspiration from all sources, and represented all artistic trends.

His faithfulness to nature and his Naturalism were revealed in 1877 in *L'Age d'airan* (*The Bronze Age*), his first exhibited work. Then, *La Porte de l'Enfer* (*The Gate of Hell*), inspired by Dante's *Divine Comedy*, commissioned in 1880 - for a Museum of Decorative Arts planned on the present site of the Orsay Museum - was the fruit of more than thirty years' work. Topped by *Les Trois Ombres* (*The Three Shades*), framed by the figures of *Adam* and *Eve*, this gigantic gate epitomises Rodin's work in the body movement's expressivity, the cult devoted to nudity, and the fluidity or brutality of his modelling. Most of his figures were exhibited separately, as, for example, *Le Penseur* (*The Thinker*) in 1880, *Le Baiser* (*The Kiss*) and *Fugit Amor* in 1880-1882, or *Ugolino* in 1882, whose totally Romantic pathos is reminiscent of Barye and Carpeaux.

Like all the sculptors of his age, Rodin worked on public monuments: *Les Bourgeois de Calais* (*The Burghers of Calais*), begun in 1884 and the statue of *Victor Hugo* of 1889, glorified national heroes.

His talent as a portraitist may be seen in his innumerable busts of writers and artists: Henri Rochefort, Puvis de Chavannes or Jules Dalou. His busts of women, *Madame Vicuna* and *La Pensée* (*Thought*) of 1888 bear witness to Symbolist research in his contrasting smooth forms and uncut marble. Finally, in his statue of Balzac that created such an uproar at the 1898 Salon, one is struck by his distorted and exaggerated modelling. Rodin conveyed reality not by imitating it, "but in magnifying, in exaggerating the holes and the bosses." With this work he attained an Expressionist force which would evolve in the XXth century.

new idea of an "art for everybody": objects
and ornaments were industrially mass-pro-
duced, at most widely-accessible prices.
In Brussels, the Tassel Hotel and the home
of Octave Aubecq, built respectively in 1892
and 1899-1904 by Victor Horta, were very
early illustrations of this harmony between
architecture and its decoration, running
through its woodwork to its furniture; in
1893, Henry Van de Velde constructed, decorated and furnished his house in Uccle.
In France, "art's architect" Hector Guimard, one of the movement's major representatives together with Emile Gallé, designed the wrought-iron entrances to the
Parisian underground railways, benches,
railings, window-boxes and balconies
abounding in characteristic arabesqued and
assymetrical plant motifs.
The Nancy School was centred around decorator and cabinet-maker Louis Majorelle
and, above all, glassmaker Emile Gallé who
was also a manufacturer of "sculpted and
inlaid wooden furniture." Their inspiration
was drawn from nature: lotus flowers, waterlilies, convolvulus and orchids graced
furniture, lamps, ceramics and crystal vases.
Several rooms at the Orsay Museum display
Art Nouveau's wealth of individual techniques and the originality of each artist:
Jean Dampt's panelling, Alexandre Charpentier's dining-room, François-Rupert
Carabin's bookcase, Louis Comfort Tiffany
and Eugène Grasset's stained-glass windows, René Lalique and Eugène Feuil-
lâtre's jewellery. Chairs from the Austrian
firm Thonet or Scotsman Charles Rennie
Mackintosh, and architectural elements
from the American Sullivan reveal the outstanding originality of the Vienna, Glasgow
and Chicago Schools.
Thus, on the middle level of the museum,
the visitor may follow artistic development
during the IIIrd Republic, remarkable for its
triumphant official art, inspired from history or Naturalism, which is then contrasted
by the emergence of independent movements towards the beginning of the XXth
century.

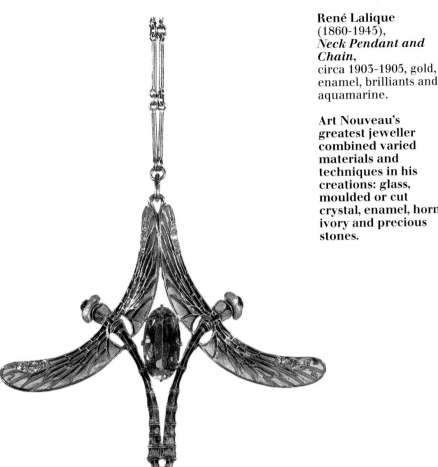

René Lalique
(1860-1945),
Neck Pendant and Chain,
circa 1903-1905, gold, enamel, brilliants and aquamarine.

Art Nouveau's greatest jeweller combined varied materials and techniques in his creations: glass, moulded or cut crystal, enamel, horn, ivory and precious stones.

A new glass age

Art Nouveau found one its most remarkable outlets in glass-work. Henri Cros, Albert Dammousse, François Décorchemont, Louis Comfort Tiffany, and above all, Emile Gallé and the Daum brothers were among the most famous glass-makers and were at the same time artists, craftsmen and occasionally manufacturers. All domains - interior decoration, household articles, objets d'art, even jewellery - bore witness to a wealth of creativity and a renewal of techniques and sources of inspiration.

Thus, stained-glass, produced from cartoons by painters, or-namentists and designers like Albert Besnard, Eugène Grasset and Jacques Grüber, was an important element in the decoration of Art Nouveau houses. The American Louis Comfort Tiffany invented Favrile glass, a coloured blown glass with an opalescent surface, and in 1895 exhibited stained-glass windows taken from paintings by Pierre Bonnard and Henri Toulouse-Lautrec. Henri Cros created a fountain in paste to adorn the Luxembourg Museum.

Technical experiments undertaken by Emile Gallé were among the most innovative. Head of an industrial applied arts school, known as the Nancy School, Gallé sought the subtlest processes, colours, forms and decoration: blown, crackled, marbled glass and crystal, inlaid work, iridescence and transparency; frosted, engraved, enamelled, painted or gilded decoration with metal inlays. His vases took their names from Verlaine and Baudelaire's poems, while the cup *Par une telle nuit* (*On Such a Night*) in 1894 was a phrase borrowed from a Berlioz opera. Plant and animal motifs invaded the surface of his creations, as in *Liseron d'octobre* (*Autumn Convolvulus*) in 1891, *Fleurs d'oi-gnons* (*Onion Flowers*) in 1900, and *La Main aux algues et aux coquillages* (*Hand with Seaweed and Shells*) in 1904. From 1890 onwards, Gallé's work influenced glassmaker and jeweller René Lalique. He inserted moulded or engraved crystal between the enamels and precious stones of his jewellery, and experimented with new techniques, especially the lost wax process for decoration on the inside of his works. In their refined research, these glass-makers sought a harmony of form and decoration, an essential principle of Art Nouveau.

Emile Gallé (1846-1904),
Autumn Convolvulus, 1891, crystal vase in two layers, inlays, engraved decoration, base in cut and engraved crystal, 18 cm.
The title of this vase recalls a line from Verlaine, "You have stooped over my melancholy." The elegance of the crystal, its technique and decoration bear witness to the masterly skill of the Nancy School.

Hector Guimard
(1867-1942),
Double Door, 1897, walnut, elm, wrought iron and copper, 364 × 120 cm.

The only remaining element from the conversion of an Angers gunsmith's shop, this door illustrates the "Guimard style" with its interweaving vertical lines and sinuous arabesques in wood and iron.

Alexandre Charpentier

Alexandre
Charpentier
(1856-1909)
Both technically and
artistically versatile,
Alexandre
Charpentier was a
sculptor, medal-
maker, pewterer,
cabinet- maker,
embosser and
chaser. He
embodied Art
Nouveau's artist-
craftsman: his
decorative suites, his
furniture, his bas-
reliefs and
household objects
brought art into the
everyday
surroundings of
private life. He also
created works like
Hawkins' Mask in
1893, which
expressed a
Symbolist tendency.

Dining-room for the villa of banker Adrien Bénard at Champrosay

circa 1900, mahogany, oak and poplar, gilded bronzes, fountain and stoneware tiles by Alexandre Bigot
3.46 × 10.55 × 6.21 m

A rare, almost complete interior décor, this dining-room illustrates Art Nouveau's search for unity between the arts, a then revolutionary concept: architecture, sculpture, ceramics, bronze and furniture.

Alexandre Charpentier trained as a sculptor, but was also a decorator, chaser and cabinet-maker who rejected eclecticism's disparate influences and overladen style, and created new forms whose sinuous lines were drawn from plant life. He adapted the arrangement of this dining-room to the space at his disposal. The room is thus divided by a beam supported by two metal columns; Charpentier designed two sculpted pillars rising from which is a purely decorative central arch that seems, however, to sustain this beam. Two console-sideboards, two silver cabinets and a fountain are built into the woodwork running above which are the stiles and a glazed stoneware-tiled frieze. The table, which originally included twenty-four chairs, was also the product of Charpentier's imagination. A chandelier and wall-lights completed the décor. In its harmonious materials of oak, poplar and mahogany, bronze and stoneware, in its expansive forms and fluid décor, this dining-room exemplifies Art Nouveau. It was commissioned by banker Adrien Bénard, in charge of the Parisian underground railway construction programme, and a staunch defender of the works of Hector Guimard. At the turn of the century in France, Art Nouveau's clientele came from the rising middle class, made up of industrialists and financiers, who, to affirm their position in society, wished to have their mansions and villas decorated by modern artists: Jean Dampt, Rupert Carabin, Hector Guimard and Alexandre Charpentier.

Proust, fin-de-siècle observer

In 1892, Marcel Proust, twenty-one years of age, sat for Jacques-Emile Blanche. "There was more of the schoolboy he had scarcely left behind about him than the dandy he wished to become. His dandified attire was already out-of-date, being in the Batignolles style that Manet's model for *Père Lathuile* wore, George Moore's studied untidiness, with a certain schoolboyish affectation of keeping one's gloves on to hide one's ink-stained fingers," recalled the society portraitist. Sixteen years later, in 1908, Proust began his vast work *A la Recherche du temps perdu.*

Paris was then the undisputed capital of European aestheticism. Dilettantism, decadence and dandyism, Symbolism and idealism, subtilism and conversationism, pessimism and cynicism, snobism, idleness and frivolity, anglomania and cosmopolitanism, elegance, preciosity and extravagance: so many words used to describe the fashionable, aristocratic, artistic and literary figures of the years 1880-1914.

In his novel Proust brings to life the climate at the turn of the century, the elegance of the Faubourg Saint-Germain, this "emanation of a small number of people who propel him to a quite distant degree [...] into the circle of their friends and friends of their friends whose names form a sort of repertory." Between the real characters, known or perceived by the writer, and those he created in his book, an impressive portrait gallery is built up, in which the world and demi-monde, painters and writers reflect the sensibility of an era, its trends and tastes, its political events, such as the Dreyfus Affair that was to split French opinion.

Proust frequented fashionable Paris in Mme Emile Strauss and Madeleine Lemaire's elegant Salons, or those of Countess Grefflhe and Méry Laurent, among the editorial staff of *La Revue blanche*, and at cafés or restaurants in vogue. He met Stéphane Mallarmé, Anatole France, and Alphonse Daudet. He admired the painting of Monet, Renoir, Paul Helleu and James Whistler, listened to Richard Wagner and Gabriel Fauré, and applauded Réjane and Sarah Bernhardt. Some of the heroes in *La Recherche* were based on high society figures. Dandy Charles Haas was the model for Charles Swann and Count Robert de Montesquiou inspired the character of Baron Charlus. Patron and poet, "nutrient medium for microbes of frivolity" according to writer Gustave Kahn, Montesquiou was one of the Belle Epoque's most famous personalities and a source of inspiration for writers, painters and sculptors. He was Des Esseintes, hero of Joris-Karl Huysmans' Symbolist novel, or "breviary of decadence", *A Rebours*, in 1884. He was also Oscar Wilde's *Dorian Grey* in 1891. Giovanni Boldini brilliantly portrayed this prince among aesthetes in 1897, and Paul Troubetzkoy cast him in bronze in 1907.

The society portraits exhibited in the Orsay Museum both recall the universe of Marcel Proust and bear witness to the fin-de-siècle atmosphere in Paris.

Giovanni Boldini (1842-1931),
Robert de Montesquiou, 1897,
oil on canvas, 116 × 82 cm.
Count Robert de Montesquiou-Fezensac embodied the Belle Epoque's affected dandyism. "I should no longer call myself anything but Montesproust," he said, offended, when he recognised himself in Baron Charlus, one of Marcel Proust's characters.

Head inset:
Jacques-Emile Blanche (1861-1942),
Portrait of Marcel Proust, 1892,
oil on canvas, 75 × 60 cm.
The literary and society portrait enjoyed a huge success; with John Singer Sargent, Antonio de La Gandara and Giovanni Boldini, Jacques-Emile Blanche made it his speciality and painted all the intellectual personalities of the turn of the century.

ITINERARY
'5

Exploration

- The cinema, a première
- Gauguin's islands of paradise
- Bonnard, the "Nabi japonard"
- The Viennese *Sezession*: in search of a "total art"
- Towards Expressionism

Discoveries

- Cezanne's *Woman with a Coffee Pot*
- Matisse's *Luxury, Calm and Delight*
- Douanier Rousseau's *The Snake Charmer*
- Maillol's *The Mediterranean*

Encounter with

- The Natansons, founders of *la Revue Blanche*

On the tracks of the XXth century (1900-1914)

by Marina Ferretti-Bocquillon

With the evolution of Art Nouveau, the last years of the XIXth century saw the dawning of new decorative ambitions and the idea of a "total art", through which artists meant to transform the everyday environment. The new techniques of a century that invented photography, the cinema and also reinforced concrete opened up fresh territories for creators in search of modernity.

The actual beginning of XXth century artistic history was in 1905, a year that paid homage to the Post-Impressionists who became the XXth century "Primitives".

The hanging of the exhibits in the Orsay Museum highlights the "key works" that guided young generations at the turn of the century. Painters active in the XIXth century, but who would lead a brilliant career in the XXth century, such as Bonnard and the Nabis, also hold a place of honour. Other works are those of artists who, still in their youth, would soon take part in avant-garde artistic movements: a Mondrian landscape, a "Neo-Impressionist" Matisse...

1900

Art Nouveau triumphed at the Paris Exposition Universelle. First section of the Parisian underground railway decorated by Guimard. Construction of Orsay Station, the Grand and Petit Palais and Alexander III Bridge. Picasso's first stay in Paris.

1901

Picasso Exhibition at Vollard's. Death of Toulouse-Lautrec.

1902

Stieglitz founded *Photo Secession*. Death of Zola. Van de Velde head of industrial art workshops in Weimar.

1903

Death of Gauguin, Pissarro and Whistler. Stieglitz launched the review *Camera Work*. Closure of the *Revue Blanche*.

1905

Van Gogh and Seurat retrospectives at the Salon des Artistes Indépendants. Formation of German "Die Brucke" group, prelude to European Expressionism. "Fauve" scandal at the Salon d'Automne.

1906

Death of Paul Cézanne. Gauguin retrospective at the Salon d'Automne.

1907

Cézanne retrospective at the Salon d'Automne. Picasso completed *Les Demoiselles d'Avignon*.

1908

Braque and Picasso's first Cubist landscapes.

1909

Marinetti published the first *Manifesto of Futurism*.

1910

Kandinsky's first abstract work. Death of Douanier Rousseau.

1914

First World War.

Artistic history of the XXth century began in 1905, one of those pivotal years when all the elements that would have a lasting effect on the era suddenly fell into place. The Van Gogh and Seurat retrospectives at the Salon des Indépendants set the tone: the Post-Impressionists became the XXth century "Primitives." In the adjoining rooms, Munch exhibited *The Kiss* and Matisse *Luxe, Calme et Volupté (Luxury, Calm and Delight)*, a free adaptation of Neo-Impressionist technique. A few months later, at the Salon d'Automne, Matisse presented his decidedly Fauvist works that marked the emergence of the avant-garde movements.

While the Fauvist painters caused a furor at the Salon, they shared the limelight with the former Nabis and Maillol, who exhibited the model for *The Mediterranean*, his first large sculpture proclaiming his return to a classical style. The same year, Picasso abandoned the melancholic Expressionism of his blue period: 1907 saw the completion of the *Demoiselles d'Avignon* and the Cézanne retrospective. In 1909, the poet Marinetti published the first Futurist manifesto, and, the following year, Kandinsky painted his first abstract work. The foundations of XXth century art were laid.

Post-Impressionism: XXth century origins

When Matisse and his friends created a scandal at the Salon d'Automne, their paintings, whose brushwork and colours were expressed with a fierce intensity, earned them the nickname of "Fauves" (wild cats) from critic Louis Vauxelles, and were likened to " a pot of paint thrown into the public's face." But despite their violence, these works sprang directly from Post-Impressionist research: Vlaminck declared his affiliation with Van Gogh; in 1904, Matisse tried his hand at Neo-Impressionism

Vincent Van Gogh
(1853-1890),
The Italian Woman,
1887,
oil on canvas,
81 × 60 cm.

From Delacroix to the Fauves, the theme of the exotic woman revealed an escapist longing. Here, the face is reduced to a mask, while the medley of red and green on the dress stands out brilliantly against the sunlit background.

Paul Cézanne

La Femme à la cafetière
(Woman with a Coffee Pot)

circa 1890-1895
oil on canvas, 130.5 × 96.5 cm.

Paul Cézanne
(1839-1906)
A friend of Zola in
his youth, Cézanne
enrolled at the Swiss
Academy in 1861.
There he met
Pissarro with whom
he was to abandon
his early sombre,
impasto style (*La
Madeleine - Mary
Magdalen*, circa
1869). A measured
Impressionism may
be seen in *La
Maison du pendu*
(*The House of the
Hanged Man*) of
1873, which evolved
into a more
geometric
expression (*Le Pont
de Maincy - The
Bridge at Maincy*,
circa 1879). His
favourite themes
were still-lifes,
landscapes and
women bathing. At
the end of his life,
his views of the
Sainte-Victoire
mountain attained
an increasingly
dense and compact
expression, vibrant
with colour.

The model's identity remains questionable: it has been suggested that she was the painter's mother, Madame Cézanne, or his wife, Hortense Fiquet, or even a servant of Jas de Bouffan... No matter: it is neither a portrait nor a psychological study of the sitter. *La Femme à la cafetière* (*Woman with a Coffee Pot*) goes far beyond individual expression and attains a hieratic monumentality. Her closed face is expressionless, revealing neither emotion nor personality. Her geometrized forms are treated in the same way as a still-life and are harmonious with those of the cup and coffee pot. "Nature should be treated in cylinders, spheres and cones," said Cézanne whose approach to space was identical: emphatic geometry for the door's orthogonal mouldings, frontality of a background strictly parallel to the canvas. The limited colours, applied in close, oblique brushstrokes, stress still further the composition's overall rigour, even if, occasionally, they possess the lightness of watercolours. Cézanne, who had long since distanced himself from the Impressionists, clearly appears here as "the primitive of a new art." His Post-Impressionist landscapes would have a direct influence on Braque and Picasso's first Cubist works in 1908. *La Femme à la cafetière* (*Woman with a Coffee Pot*) foreshadowed Cubism's two founders' series of figures with or without musical instruments of 1910-1914. Both the latter and this painting of Cézanne's depict large, solitary figures set in a confined space, with an assertive geometry and limited palette. Cézanne's deliberate indifference to conveying his model's individuality is only equalled by that of the Cubists, who were then bordering on abstraction.

that led up to his explosion of colours in 1905, and Derain's mosaical brushwork indicated his knowledge of Seurat's theories. Like Gauguin, they were interested in primitive objets d'art and used a wild language. They were not alone. In creating *Les Demoiselles d'Avignon*, Picasso drew inspiration from the most varied sources: African masks seen at the Trocadéro Museum, Iberian art, Gauguin's sculptures and Cézanne's painting.

Following the Cézanne retrospective at the Salon d'Automne, most painters adopted, more or less superficially, the tones and the rigour of the Aix master. In 1907, the Fauves themselves darkened their palette: Matisse and Derain produced more peaceful-coloured paintings. Braque spent the summer at l'Estaque where he renounced the vivid hues of his Fauvist canvases, limited himself to the blue-green-ochres of Cézanne's landscapes, and reduced nature to a more geometric expression that firmly structured space... Cubism was not far off.

The call of the Mediterranean

Cézanne, Van Gogh and Signac had been attracted to Mediterranean shores by the light and colour of southern France's landscapes. In 1904, Matisse used pure colour with Signac in Saint-Tropez. The following summer, he stayed with Derain at Collioure, where he did three studies for *La Joie de Vivre* (*The Joy of Living*). Maillol was not far away, in Banyuls. From then on, the movement grew and derived its strength from a deeper desire to go back to original sources.

The taste for Arcadian landscapes that had appeared in the last years of the XIXth century foreshadowed a return to a pure, balanced style influenced by early Mediterranean Antiquity. Sculptors readopted the ideals of ancient statuary. In 1905, Maillol, whose Nabi period paintings had already shown a radical simplification of form, ex-

Edgar Degas,
(1834-1917),
At the Milliner's,
circa 1898,
pastel, 91 × 75 cm.

Hats like coloured balloons fall into place and create a singular composition.

Edouard Vuillard
(1868-1940),
Profile of a Woman in a Green Hat,
circa 1891,
oil on cardboard,
21 × 16 cm.

Neither the humour of the caricatural profile, nor the success of a composition entirely built up in flat areas of colour, is spoilt by the latter's refinement.

Maurice Denis (1870-1945), *Sunlight on the Terrace,* 1890, oil on cardboard, 24 × 20.5 cm.

A revealing vision from the first artist to state that a painting "before being a war-horse, a nude woman or banal anecdote, is essentially a flat surface covered in colours assembled in a certain order."

Henri-Edmond Cross (1856-1910), *The Golden Isles (The Hyères Isles),* 1891-1892, oil on canvas, 59 × 54 cm.

The landscape of the South of France reduced to the compenetration of colours. Dotted brushstrokes unite the surface: only the decrescent size of the coloured spots suggests distance.

Henri Matisse

Henri Matisse
(1869-1954)
Matisse discovered
painting while
confined to bed by
illness. He
consequently gave
up his career as a
solicitor's clerk,
enrolled at the
Julian Academy in
1892, and at the
Ecole des Beaux-
Arts, where he
frequented Gustave
Moreau's studio. In
1905, he painted *La
Femme au chapeau*
which was the chief
attraction in the
room dedicated to
the Fauves at the
Salon d'Automne
that year. He evolved
towards a more
controlled expression,
in which space was
dominated by
intense colours cut
up by the sinuous
arabesques of his
drawing (*La Desserte
rouge* - Red
Harmony, 1908). He
rapidly appeared as
one of the major
figures of XXth
century art, travelled
extensively, from
Biskra, in Algeria, to
Tahiti. At the end of
his life, Matisse
created vast
compositions made
up of cut-out,
coloured paper (*La
Tristesse du roi*).

Luxe, calme et volupté
(Luxury, Calm and Delight)
1904
oil on canvas, 98 × 118 cm.

Famous landmark on the way from fin-de-siècle painting to XXth century art, this brilliant canvas illustrates the affiliation linking Fauvism to Neo-Impressionism. The contradiction between a scientific approach to colour and the violent expression of Fauvist works is resolved here by Matisse, who uses Neo-Impressionist theories with evident ease to obtain maximum depth of colour. Matisse spent the summer of 1904 at Paul Signac's in Saint-Tropez. He had read *From Eugène Delacroix to Neo-Impressionism*, published in 1899, in which Signac developed, in his treatise on Neo-Impressionist theories, an impassioned cult to colour. This handbook was read by a whole generation of painters, who, for the most part, tried their hand, however briefly, at Neo-Impressionism. On his dining-room walls in Saint-Tropez, Signac had hung a painting of his friend Cross, *L'Air du soir* (*Evening Breeze*) that also evoked "the Eden of Saint-Tropez." Matisse adopted the same theme and attempted the rigorous Divisionist technique. The fragmented brushstrokes he used here were abandoned immediately afterwards, but the violence of his colours survived in the Fauvist works he exhibited at the 1905 Salon d'Automne. Under the spell of the Mediterranean landscape, with *Luxe, calme et volupté* Matisse found the original motif for *La Joie de vivre* that he was to develop the following year in Collioure, and which would be one of the recurrent themes of his works. The painting's title, taken from a line of Baudelaire, conveys his search for a golden age "where there is only order and beauty, luxury, calm and delight." Anxious to situate Neo-Impressionism in a historical perspective, Signac immediately grasped the importance of this work, which he bought at the 1905 Salon des Indépendants, and that he chose to hang opposite *Evening Breeze*. Today, at the Orsay Museum, the visitor may still compare these two paintings which are at the same time so close, yet so different.

Paul Cézanne
(1839-1906)
Rocks near the Caves above the Château Noir, circa 1904, oil on canvas, 65 × 54 cm.

Cézanne's dense, rigorous, lyrical space: rocks and air, tree-trunks and foliage are submitted to a uniform treatment of coloured brushstrokes.

Ferdinand Hodler
(1853-1918),
Schynige Platte. Oberland Landscape, 1909, oil on canvas, 67 × 90.5 cm.

A landscape taken to the threshold of abstraction through its strict frontality and the horizontal cutting up of the mountain into coloured strips. All the poetry of a composition both reminiscent of Neo-Impressionism and influenced by Japanese art.

Maurice de Vlaminck (1876-1958), *Restaurant de la Machine at Bougival*, circa 1905, oil on canvas, 80 × 81.5 cm.

Fauvist variation on an Impressionist theme. Van Gogh-like brushwork and colours.

André Derain (1880-1954) *Charing Cross Bridge*, circa 1906, oil on canvas, 81 × 100 cm.

A work representative of Derain's Fauvist period: freedom of colour and treatment applied to an Impressionist theme.

Pierre Bonnard (1897-1947), *The Box*, 1908, oil on canvas, 91 × 120 cm.

A commissioned work that has none of the society portrait: while the lighting illuminates the womens' beauty, the insolence of a Degas-type viewpoint erases the faces of the men.

Henri Rousseau, known as le Douanier Rousseau

Henri Rousseau, known as le Douanier Rousseau (1844-1910) A Paris toll-collector from 1870 to 1883, he retired at forty, and began painting. He created landscapes, portraits of his family and close friends (*La Carriole du père Jugnier - Père Jugnier's Cart*, 1900) or imaginary scenes (*La Guerre - War* in 1894 and *La Bohémienne endormie - The Sleeping Gypsy* in 1897). Rousseau never travelled. He transfigured the exotic vegetation seen in the Jardin des Plantes and worked from photographs or popular illustrations. His oneiric and naive universe fascinated both Apollinaire and Picasso.

La Charmeuse de serpents
(The Snake Charmer)
1907
oil on canvas, 169 × 189.5 cm.

To help his friend le Douanier, painter Robert Delauney suggested his mother commission Rousseau to do a work inspired by her exotic accounts of her stay in India. This was how le Douanier Rousseau, who had never travelled, produced this astonishing evocation of an imaginary jungle, and found his necessary inspiration in the Botanical Gardens in Paris, the Jardin des Plantes. Charmed by a wild, mysterious Eve's nocturnal melody are animals that live in the luxuriant vegetation studiously depicted by the artist. The density of the forest is contrasted with the space on the left, occupied by an empty sky and the stretch of water that reflects the moon's pale luminosity.

The evocative power of the work springs essentially from the dreamlike atmosphere of this scene bathed in moonlight: the improbable harmony between animals and nature, the sorceress Eve's strong figure, together with the music conjured up by her flute. No movement breaks the mystery of this image in which time is miraculously suspended. The radical flattening of forms and the play on black and green create a climate of unreality. This poetic force aroused great enthusiasm among Rousseau's painter and writer friends. Gauguin, Apollinaire and Picasso in particular liked "primitive" Rousseau's sincerity. In 1905, Picasso organised a banquet at the Bateau-Lavoir in his honour. The painting's oneiric dimension also charmed the Surrealists, for it was André Breton who encouraged fashion designer Jacques Doucet to buy it from Robert Delaunay in 1922. The latter only accepted to part with the painting on condition that it would be bequeathed to the Louvre on the collector's death. Which it was.

hibited his model for *The Mediterranean,* a sculpture overtly classical in inspiration. While Rodin, the undisputed master, produced works of an increasingly tormented nature, Bourdelle was drawn to a simple style tinged with archaism, as may be seen in the balanced volumes, formal purity and strength of his *Heraklès archer* (*Heracles the Bowman*).

Each artist found his own primitive source: Maurice Denis, impressed by the works of Fra Angelico, moved towards painting of religious inspiration and rediscovered the aesthetic values of XVth century Tuscany. From 1899 onwards, this new orientation appeared in the decoration of the Sainte-Croix Chapel at Vésinet. Bonnard, Vuillard and Roussel also executed vast decorative panels, whose themes were often taken from Mediterranean myths and legends. As in their paintings, space was organised in juxtaposed zones of colour, with no attempt made to create an illusion of depth that would hollow out the wall. In 1911, Bonnard completed his triptych *Mediterranean* for the house entrance of the famous collector Morosov in Moscow. His painting evolved into very personal work on colour that in certain aspects heralded American abstract art of the 1950s, and through its colourful lyricism converged with his friend Monet's *Nymphéas* (*Waterlilies*).

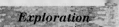

Gauguin's islands
of paradise

Bonnard,
the "Nabi japonard"

Pierre Bonnard, (1897-1947),
The Game of Croquet, 1892, oil on canvas, 130 × 162 cm.
The artist's family and friends submitted to a very "japonard"
exercise: decorative use of fabrics, flattened vegetation,
distorted silhouettes (the dog) and sinuous lines.

Gauguin, proud of his Peruvian origins and his "Indian profile," dreamed of escape in slightly Romantic terms. He wanted to leave European civilisation behind and rediscover the "savage" within him. After a stay in Panama and Martinique in 1887, he spent long hours at the 1889 Exposition Universelle. This time exoticism was to be found in Paris. At the foot of the Eiffel Tower there were villages peopled by authentic natives. The Javanese dancers impressed him the most. Gauguin imagined having a "tropical studio" and chose Tahiti. When he arrived on the island in 1891, the missionaries had long since got the better of local cults and customs, and the Tahitians wore European dress. Native

objets d'art were scarce: they were all in the museum. Gauguin painted and sculpted what he had dreamed of finding: dense, floral vegetation, half-naked natives, mysterious idols. His colours were as "barbaric" as possible, his forms strong and simple, inspired from all kinds of "primitive" art: Egyptian, Javanese and Peruvian... Gauguin transposed his "imaginary museum." In 1890, in Brittany, he had already produced a polychrome, wooden bas-relief that was Tahitian in aspect. Forms were boldly simplified under the evocative title of *Soyez mystérieuses* (*Be Mysterious*). Clearly Gauguin had already been dreaming of Tahiti. When this strange sculpture featured in the 1906 retrospective at the Salon d'Automne, it must have caught the attention of the most audacious young painters. In search of formal innovation, XXth century artists looked in turn towards primitive arts, which became an essential source of their inspiration: Matisse and Picasso collected masks and fetishes; the Fauves, followed by the Expressionists, saw in these objects the expression of a basic impulse.

Paul Gauguin, (1848-1903),
Oviri, 1894, partially enamelled ceramic stoneware,
75 × 19 × 27 cm.
One of Gauguin's last ceramics, executed in Paris, after his first trip to Tahiti. Called "the killer" by Gauguin, he wished to have her placed on his grave. Oviri, the Tahitian word for "wild", was also a god of death in the island's primitive mythology.

In 1890, an exhibition of Japanese prints was held at the Ecole des Beaux-Arts: it was determinant for the Nabis who all advocated an art with simplified forms and adopted the flat areas of colour characteristic of Japanese prints. Not without a certain humour, Bonnard deliberately made the Japanese style his own: he was very "japonard." In *L'Enfant au Seau* (*Child with a Bucket*) or *Le Peignoir* (*The Dressing-gown*), he adopted the elongated format of the kakemono, a Japanese wall-picture, sinuous drawing and Japanese taste for decorative motifs. He especially liked spare compositions, in which zones of neutral colours alternated with empty areas. But he soon renounced this strict Japanism that nevertheless suited both the Nabis' decorative ambitions and his own talent as a lithographer and poster designer. At the turn of the century, he took a more personal direction. His colours gradually became richer and denser. Bonnard recalled his discovery of the South of France, in 1906, like "something out of the Arabian

Nights," during his stay in Saint-Tropez at the house of his painter friend, Henri-Charles Manguin. His themes (landscapes, his companion Marthe washing, interior scenes and still-lifes) were those of the Impressionists. Their reassuring charm and attractive colours could have masked the innovations in his painting. But, though Bonnard worked outside of avant-garde movements and their provocations, one finds in his works, beyond an astonishing freedom of colour, a radically new space in which his flat colours are built up in abstract fashion. The multiple viewpoints to which he submits the objects presented on any one canvas are reminiscent of Cubist or Matisse's paintings. The fabulous, shimmering colours cannot conceal the audacity of a composition that renounces classical perspective as well as the "focalisation" of a subject against a background. Here, one's gaze wanders freely over canvases that herald Jackson Pollock and American painting of the 1950s.

How the patriarch of Giverny opened the way to abstraction

In 1890, Monet began his series of *Meules* (*Haystacks*), in which he systematically adopted the same motif while attempting to capture the variety of atmospheric and light "effects." Other series were to follow: poplars, then Rouen cathedral in 1892-1893. Composition gradually faded away, as did the subject, rendered insignificant through repetition, while colour gained an extraordinary power. Kandinsky, who attained abstraction in the course of a series of landscapes that he called "impressions" and "improvisations" recalls in *Regards sur le passé* the shock received at the sight of one of Monet's *Haystacks*: "And, for the first time, I saw a picture [...]. I felt confusedly that the subject matter was absent [...]. It gave the painting a fabulous force and brilliance." Malevitch underwent a similar experience in front of the series on *Rouen Cathedral*.

In 1900, the "Patriarch of Giverny" still had a quarter of a century to explore the blue-toned universe of his water garden. Prior to this, he had created his ornamental lake by diverting the course of the River Ru, a tributary of the River Epte, had installed Japanese footbridges and grown waterlilies. During the last thirty years of his life, the artist produced over 200 panels, at times huge, in which water, plants and sky mingled together in an informal game of reflections and patches of colour. Less and less "objective", Monet's vision became lyrical, as his entangled and sinuous brushwork left long trails of colour on the surface of the canvas. The panels exhibited at the Orangerie were conceived as a coloured environment, an infinite canvas that would submerge the spectator in the painter's blue-green universe. Not far from the large studio at Giverny, the presence of the water garden somehow came to justify these canvases that herald the abstract Expressionism of a Pollock. For however beautiful it may have been, the garden at Giverny hardly

Claude Monet (1840-1926), *Rouen Cathedral. The Portal, Morning Sun (Harmony in Blue)*, 1893, oil on canvas, 91 × 65 cm.

Claude Monet, *Rouen Cathedral. The Portal and Saint Romain Tower, Full Sunlight (Harmony in Blue and Gold)*, 1893, oil on canvas, 107 × 73 cm.

"*Rouen Cathedral* is of capital importance in the history of art and forces whole generations to change their conceptions" (Malévitch).

Claude Monet,
(1840-1926),
Blue Waterlilies,
circa 1916-1919,
oil on canvas,
200 × 200 cm.

The freedom and
lyricism of Monet's
highly coloured
universe: it matters
little where
reflection ends and
reality begins.

Odilon Redon
(1840-1916),
Tree against Yellow Background. Decorative Panel at the Château de Domecy,
1901, mixed technique on canvas, 249 × 185 cm.

Redon chose the colour when trying his hand at dining-room decoration. Half-real, half-imaginary vegetation and magical, mysterious, coloured efflorescences.

Edouard Vuillard
(1868-1940),
The Chapel at Versailles, 1917-1919, oil on paper mounted on canvas, 96 × 66 cm.

The unity of texture and rich colours softens the contrast of classical architecture and the opulent head of hair.

offered the chromatic wealth and density of the works it inspired. In their atypical and varied sizes, the *Nymphéas (Waterlilies)* challenged the XIXth century idea of easel painting, and thus echoed the vast decorative compositions of Bonnard, Vuillard and Roussel.

The *Nymphéas (Waterlilies)*, like the large panels of the ex-Nabis and Odilon Redon, responded to a widespread aspiration present at the turn of the century: to give painting back its decorative ambition. By refusing to isolate a painting in a frame and to add depth to the flat surface of a canvas or a wall, artists coincided with the general leaning of the era towards the integration of painting into the everyday environment and the breaking down of excessive barriers between the different forms of artistic expression. Artists took an interest in all fields of plastic arts, an objective amply met by Art Nouveau, the great success of the 1900 Exposition Universelle, and also expressed in the works of Mackintosh – architect, decor-

The Viennese *Sezession:*
in search of "a total art"

Pierre Bonnard
(1867-1947),
Portrait of the
Bernheim de Villers
Brothers, **1920, oil on**
canvas,
165.5 × 155.5 cm.

Sublimated by the
colours' brilliant
intensity, the
abstract architecture
of a frontal space,
treated as a working-
drawing. In
counterpoint, the
dark, motionless
silhouettes of the
two art dealers.

In 1900, Art Nouveau was thriving in all big cities in Europe, and Vienna, together with Paris, was one of the most prestigious capitals. It was a modern town with electric tramways, pleasure boats and underground railway. Home of the most brilliant intellectuals, Vienna had just built a wide, circular, arterial road, the Ringstrasse, lined with edifices heavy in historical reference and copiously decorated. Hans Makart, the reigning official painter, was still mimicking Rubens. In reaction to this academicism, young artists advocated a new spirit stamped with modernity and simplicity. Urged by Otto Wagner, who was later to join them, the boldest among them decided to form a society: the *Sezession*, created on 3 April 1897, with Gustave Klimt as president. Its most active members included painter and designer Koloman Moser and architect Josef Hoffmann. From architecture to textiles, goldsmithery to jewellery, furniture to glassware, they produced wonders of simplicity and spareness, not once forgetting proportion or refined decoration. In Brussels, the Palais Stoclet (1905-1911), created by Josef Hoffmann who planned the interior design and decoration down to the smallest detail, was a shining example of the achievement of this "total art" defended by the Viennese *Sezession* movement. The latter's first exhibition took place in 1898 and was extremely successful. Vienna welcomed works by foreign artists such as Rodin, Puvis de Chavannes, Constantin Meunier, Segantini and Max Klinger. Viennese artists also discovered Mackintosh's creations. The Secession Pavilion, built by Olbrich in 1902, was soon to house their exhibitions. The simple geometry of its architecture combining spheres and squares and the elegance of its decoration sum up the spirit of this Viennese School. Its geometrical rigour foreshadowed functionalist aesthetics of the years to come.

Gustave Klimt (1862-1918),
Roses under Trees, circa 1905,
oil on canvas, 110 × 110 cm.
Characteristic refinement and modernity of the Viennese
School. The tapestry effect of the coloured brushstrokes
obliterates the landscape. Only the tree trunks
remain identifiable.

Towards
Expressionism

Expressionism developed essentially in Northern Europe from 1905 onwards, the year the German Die Brucke Group formed and the Fauves made their loud entrance at the Salon d'Automne. An expression of life's hardship, of rebellion or suffering, this artistic trend dis-

Edvard Munch (1863-1944),
Summer Night at Aagaarstand, 1904,
oil on canvas, 99 × 103.5 cm.
Insistent perspective, geometrical simplification
of the landscape, cold tones contrasted with red:
a pre-Fauve landscape.

torted reality with a rare violence. In the 1890s, Dutchman Vincent Van Gogh, Belgian James Ensor and the Swede, Edvard Munch, produced works that in many ways heralded the Expressionist movement. As early as 1887, Van Gogh distorted the features of his model in *L'Italienne (The Italian Woman)* and pushed colour to its maximum intensity, fearlessly using impasto. Soutine would remember this, applying the same principles to convey the mediocrity of his characters, poor puppets drowning in their bell-boy, valet or bridegroom suits. And the hallucinated dance of landscapes he painted at Céret found its source in his undulating visions of Auvers surrounding countryside. James Ensor also left us real visions. The caricatural intensity of his obtuse crowd of masks with their fixed, scarlet grins anticipated the universe of Emile Nolde or Max Beckmann. In 1893, the coloured vibrations and simplification of a face reduced to a skull made Munch's *Scream* the moving mirror of his gloom. In the early years of this century, the anguished tones of his schematic landscapes found an echo in Germany, before capturing the attention of the Fauves.

ator and designer — and in those of the Viennese *Sezession* movement. But, at the beginning of this century, as a reaction against Art Nouveau's floral exuberancy, "modernity and simplicity" was the general rule, a prelude to the purism and functionalism of the XXth century.

New techniques and XXth century art

Among the countless technical innovations of the XIXth century, the invention of photography, the cinema and reinforced concrete helped determine XXth century aesthetics. Architects responsible for the reconstruction of central Chicago, destroyed by fire in 1871, used, for the first time, an embedded steel stucture to strengthen the buildings; it was a fundamental contribution to XXth century architecture: with reinforced concrete, walls lost their supporting status to become mere partitions; windows and doors multiplied and widened. Light flooded into these skyscrapers that grew taller and taller, while their creators exploited the transparency and reflections of glass. Architect Louis Sullivan declared "form follows function," a maxim that enjoyed success throughout the XXth century. In the XIXth century, photographers had invented a new way of looking at the world, and photography continued to develop in the following century. Painters willingly used this medium, like Futurist Balla, whose works of movement in decomposition were inspired by Marey's chronophotographs. The Surrealists pounced on it, attracted by the various resources it offered: from "collage" to Man Ray's solarisations. But it was the cinema, the last of the XIXth century inventions, that was to have the most unexpected future. A scientific curiosity that became a popular attraction, Pathé and Gaumont cast their covetous eyes on it as early as 1896. The XXth century was on its way.

Thonet Brothers *Chair, Model No. 1,* bent beechwood, cane seat, 1881-1890, 93.5 × 42 × 52 cm.

Thonet Brothers *Chair, Model No. 51,* bent beechwood, cane seat, 1875-1888, 91.3 × 41.5 × 53 cm.

Michael Thonet launched his first factory in Vienna in 1849: he had developed and patented a system of manufacturing bentwood furniture which enabled him to mass-produce pieces that were beautiful, simple, strong and cheap. A Thonet chair is still an essential element in today's furnishing.

Charles Rennie Mackintosh (1868-1928), *Dressing-table and Mirror from the White Bedroom at Hous'hill,* 1904.

Glasgow School. The pure beauty of furniture designed by an architect (original white gloss-paint). Refined, geometrical forms close to the Viennese School's creations.

The cinema, a première

Clarence Hudson
White (1871-1925),
The Kiss, 1904,
platinotype,
24.7 × 14.8 cm.

Alfred Stieglitz (1864-
1946),
*New York, City of
Ambition,* 1910,
33.7 × 25.9 cm.

**A strong image of
the hungry town.
Preview of
*Metropolis.***

On 28 December 1895, the first public projection of moving pictures with admission charge was held at the Grand Café on the Boulevard des Capucines: the Lumière brothers had just invented the cinema. Far from being considered as the "seventh art," it was more of a curiosity on par with the numerous scientific toys and shows that had preceded it.

Among its distant ancestors were the shadow-theatre that had appeared in Italy during the XVIIth century, and above all the magic lantern, through which images painted on glass were projected onto a wall. It was the magic lantern that "replaced the walls' opacity with an impalpable iridescence," and made a legend of Geneviève de Brahant "like a vacillating and momentaneous stained-glass window" in Marcel Proust's boyhood universe. It was a Belgian physicist who, in 1829, gave his name to the "Plateau principle," according to which gradually differing images that succeed each other at very short intervals create the illusion of it being the same object in motion. He invented the phenakistoscope, ancestor of Emile Reynaud's 1877 praxinoscope, a scientific toy in which scenes were animated by rotating mirrors. Together with the magic lantern it was used in 1882 for public projections, known as the "optical theatre." Pantomimes of light or animated cartoons would soon delight visitors to the Musée Grévin.

For their part, Muybridge the American and Frenchman Marey took an interest in photography. In 1878, the former installed twelve cameras whose shutters triggered at half-second intervals, which enabled him to capture the successive stages of a galloping horse in motion.

Edison invented perforated film and the kinetoscope, with which he could run, but not project, a film in front of a spectator: the performance was strictly personal. Thanks to the Lumière brothers, enlarged projection of images onto a screen at last became possible. The future of the camera obscura lay wide-open.

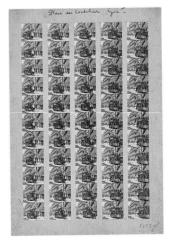

**Louis Lumière 1864-1948),
Tramways, Place des Cordeliers, Lyons,
cinematographic photogramme plate.**

Aristide Maillol

La Méditerranée
(The Mediterranean)

marble executed in 1923-1927
from the 1905 plaster model, 110 × 117 cm.

Aristide Maillol (1861-1944) Former pupil of Gérôme and Cabanel at the Ecole des Beaux- Arts, he became involved in the Nabi movement in 1893, and shared their admiration for Gauguin and Cézanne. He abandoned painting and tapestry for sculpture. The *Mediterranean* he presented at the 1905 Salon was his first large work. The same year, he met Count Kessler who became his patron. His works were essentially devoted to the female nude, whose smooth, geometrical volumes were of classical inspiration, as in *La Nuit (The Night)* of 1909, and *Harmony*, his last sculpture that remained unfinished. Several of his works may be seen in the Jardins des Tuileries.

"She is beautiful, she signifies nothing, it is a silent work," remarked Gide, when Maillol presented *The Mediterranean* at the Salon d'Automne of 1905, the year the loud Fauvist exhibition launched the avant-garde era that, from Futurist manifestations to Dadaist provocations, would witness art's noisy stage appearance. It was indeed a question of a "silent revolution." Maillol was forty when he opted for sculpture. Five years of research were necessary before he obtained the formal perfection of *The Mediterranean*, which was his first large statue. The sculptor constantly modified the balance of volumes, in search of a sparer, more geometrical harmony. The sculpture gradually took form in an ideal cube and attained this serene, smooth grandeur reminiscent of the works of Classical Greece. In his painted and woven works of the Nabi period, Maillol had already traced the motif of the timeless woman bather that would remain the central theme of his production. Commissioned in 1923, delivered by the artist in 1927, *The Mediterranean*, which was first called *Pensée, pensée latine (Thought, Latin Thought)*, was placed in the Jardin des Tuileries, where she blended harmoniously into the classical lay-out of the French garden.

The Natansons, founders of the *Revue blanche*

In 1891, when the three Natanson brothers, Alexandre, Thadée and Alfred, sons of a wealthy Russo-Polish banker, opened the Paris offices of the *Revue blanche*, it had already been in circulation for two years in Liège. At the time, new avant-garde and artistic reviews were numerous, but the *Revue blanche* rapidly became the most prestigious of them all.

It was run by Alexandre, the eldest of the three brothers, a lawyer and great art lover. He notably commissioned Vuillard's five very famous panels, *Jardins Publics* (*The Park*), for his dining-room. Alfred, the youngest, was on the editorial staff and wrote under the name of Alfred Athis. But the review's real driving force was Thadée. He and his first wife, Misia Godebska, were the centre of a circle of intellectuals and artists, who, for twelve years, filled the eclectic and impassioned columns of the *Revue blanche*.

Features in the monthly issues included poems and prose, political essays, sports, caricatures and original illustrations, art reviews and controversial editorials, especially in defence of Dreyfus. Misia, whose beauty and personality attracted the friendship of many painters and writers, inspired a profusion of portraits. A talented pianist and a friend of Debussy, Mallarmé, Bonnard and Toulouse-Lautrec, she entertained numerous celebrities at the couple's apartment in the rue Saint-Florentin, where people would meet, debates were lively and friendship

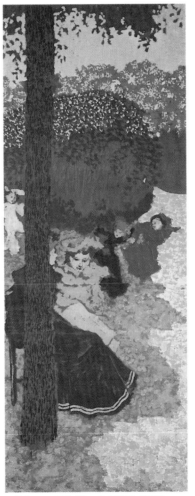

Edouard Vuillard (1868-1940),
The Park: Girls Playing,
214 × 88 cm;
one of five decorative panels, 1894.
Vuillard, like all members of the Nabi group, was attracted to decorative murals, and painted these panels for Alexandre Natanson's dining-room.

Head inset:
Edouard Vuillard (1868-1940),
Thadée Natanson (1868-1951), 1907-1908,
oil on canvas, 200 × 200.5 cm.

was encouraged. Fame of the review with the white cover spread rapidly. Counting the names of contributing authors recalls all the glory of the Belle Epoque. Stéphane Mallarmé and Paul Verlaine, but also Huysmans, Léon Blum, André Gide and Octave Mirabeau were willing *Revue* writers. The music page was signed Debussy. While Symbolism was given the place of honour among the *Revue blanche* features, the magazine also welcomed such widely-varying talents as those of Alfred Jarry, Tolstoï and Strinberg.

In 1895, Félix Fénéon, who remained the most clairvoyant art critic of his age, became the *Revue*'s assistant editor, and in fact took on the role of editor. The magazine was conspicuous in its defence of Cézanne, Gauguin, Munch and Rousseau. In 1899, the *Revue blanche* publishing house brought out Signac's book *From Eugène Delacroix to Neo-Impressionism* that had appeared in the review in serial form the previous year. In 1900, Fénéon and the Natanson's organised an extensive Seurat retrospective, on the premises of the *Revue*. But, despite the quality and originality of its articles, despite the illustrations on its frontispiece, signed by those sometimes referred to as the "Revue blanche painters," the Nabis, Bonnard, Vuillard, Denis, Vallotton and also Toulouse-Lautrec and Redon, despite a circulation of 15,000, the *Revue blanche* continued to lose money. The Natansons put an end to their venture in 1905.

For further information

Exhibition and museum catalogues

■ *Chicago, Naissance d'une métropole.* Catalogue from the exhibition at the Orsay Museum, by John Zukowsky, Henri Loyrette and Heinrick Klotz, Paris, Editions de la Réunion des Musées Nationaux, 1987.

■ *Degas.* Catalogue from the exhibition at the Grand Palais, by Jean Sutherland Boggs, Henri Loyrette, Michael Pantazzi and Gary Tinterow, Paris, Editions de la Réunion des Musées Nationaux, 1988.

■ *De Manet à Matisse, Sept ans d'enrichissements au musée d'Orsay.* Catalogue from the exhibition at the Orsay Museum, Paris, Editions de la Réunion des Musées Nationaux, 1990.

■ *Gauguin.* Catalogue from the exhibition at the Grand Palais, by Richard Bretell, Françoise Cachin, Claire Frèches-Thory and Charles F. Stuckey, Paris, Editions de la Réunion des Musées Nationaux, 1989.

■ *Gustave Courbet.* Catalogue from the exhibition at the Grand Palais, Paris, Editions de la Réunion des Musées Nationaux, Septembre 1977-January 1978.

■ *Hommage à Monet.* Catalogue from the exhibition at the Grand Palais, by Hélène Adhémar, Anne Distel and Sylvie Gache- Patin, Paris, Editions de la Réunion des Musées Nationaux, 1980.

■ *Japonisme.* Catalogue from the exhibition at the Grand Palais, by Marc Bascou, Geneviève Lacambre, Akiko Mabuchi, Caroline Mathieu and Shûji Takashima, Paris, Editions de la Réunion des Musées Nationaux, 1988.

■ *L'Art en France sous le Second Empire.* Catalogue from the exhibition at the Grand Palais, by Victor Beyer and Jean-Marie Moulin, Paris, Editions de la Réunion des Musées Nationaux, May-August 1979.

■ *Manet.* Catalogue from the exhibition at the Grand Palais, by Françoise Cachin and Charles S. Moffett, Editions de la Réunion des Musées Nationaux, 1983.

■ *Moreau-Nélaton.* Catalogue from the exhibition at the Grand Palais, by Françoise Cachin, Vincent Pomarède and Pierre Rosenberg, Paris, Editions de la Réunion des Musées Nationaux, 1991.

■ *Musée d'Orsay.* Illustrated museum catalogue of decorative arts, Paris, Editions de la Réunion des Musées Nationaux, 1988.

■ *Musée d'Orsay.* Illustrated museum catalogue of architectural and decorative art drawings, Paris, Editions de la Réunion des Musées Nationaux, 1986.

■ *Musée d'Orsay.* Illustrated museum catalogue of painters (two volumes: A-L, M-Z) Paris, Editions de la Réunion des Musées Nationaux, 1990.

■ *Musée d'Orsay.* Illustrated museum catalogue of sculptures, Paris, Editions de la Réunion des Musées Nationaux, 1986.

■ *Odilon Redon.* Catalogue from the exhibition at the Musée des Beaux-Arts. Bordeaux, 1985.

■ *Renoir.* Catalogue from the exhibition at the Grand Palais, by Anne Distel, John House and John Walsh, Jr., Paris, Editions de la Réunion des Musées Nationaux, 1985.

■ *Seurat.* Catalogue from the exhibition at the Grand Palais, by Françoise Cachin, Robert L. Herbert, Anne Distel and Gary Tinterow, Paris, Editions de la Réunion des Musées Nationaux, 1991.

■ *Sur les traces de Jean-Baptiste Carpeaux.* Catalogue from the exhibition at the Grand Palais, Paris, Editions de la Réunion des Musées Nationaux, March-May 1975.

■ *Toulouse-Lautrec.* Catalogue from the exhibition at the Grand Palais, by Claire Frèches-Thory, Anne Roquebert and Richard Thomson, Paris, Editions de la Réunion des Musées Nationaux, 1992.

■ *Van Gogh à Paris.* Catalogue from the exhibition at the Orsay Museum, by Françoise Cachin and Bogomila Welsh-Ovcharov, Paris, Editions de la Réunion des Musées Nationaux, 1988.

■ *Vienne. L'Apocalypse joyeuse.* Catalogue from the exhibition at the Pompidou Centre, Paris, 1986.

Bibliography

■ CAILLE, Marie-Thérèse: *Images des paysans*, Paris, Editions de la Réunion des Musées Nationaux, carnet Parcours No. 5, 1986.

■ CASSOU, Jean, in collaboration with Pierre Brunel, Francis Claudon, Georges Pillement and Lionel Richard: *Encyclopédie du Symbolisme*, Paris, Somogy, 1979.

■ CHAMPFLEURY, Jules: *Le Réalisme*, Paris, Hermann, 1973.

■ CROSNIER-LECONTE, Marie-Laure: *La Gare et l'hôtel d'Orsay*, Paris, Editions de la Réunion des Musées Nationaux, carnet Parcours No. 4, 1986.

■ CROSNIER-LECONTE, Marie-Laure: *Victor Laloux, L'architecte de la gare d'Orsay*, Paris, Editions de la Réunion des Musées Nationaux, Orsay Museum Dossier No. 9, 1987.

■ DELACROIX, Eugène: *Journal*, 1822-1863, Paris, Plon, 1981.

■ HEILBRUN, Françoise and NÉAGU, Philippe. *Musée d'Orsay; Chefs-d'œuvre de la collection photographique*, Paris, Philippe Sers-Editions de la Réunion des Musées Nationaux, 1986.

■ HEILBRUN, Françoise and NÉAGU, Philippe. *La photographie au musée d'Orsay. Un choix des collections.* (1839-1918). Paris. Editions de la Réunion des Musées Nationaux, Petit Journal des grandes expositions, No. 186, 1988.

■ HERBERT, Robert L.: *L'Impressionnisme: les plaisirs et les jours*, Paris. Flammarion, 1988.

■ *Histoire de l'art, Du réalisme à nos jours*, (encyclopédie de la Pléiade) by Bernard Dorival, Vol. IV, Paris, Gallimard, 1969.

■ JENGER, Jean: *Construire le musée d'Orsay*, Paris, Editions de la Réunion des Musées Nationaux, carnet Parcours No. 9, 1987.

■ JENGER, Jean: *Orsay, de la gare au musée. Histoire d'un grand projet*, Milan-Paris, Electa-Moniteur, 1986.

■ *La Méditerrannée de Maillol*. Orsay Museum Dossier, Paris, Edition de la Réunion des Musées Nationaux, 1986.

■ *La peinture au musée d'Orsay*, Paris, Edition Scala-Réunion des Musées Nationaux, 1986.

■ *La Revue du Louvre*, No. 6. Article on the opening of the Orsay Museum, Paris, 1986.

■ *Le livre de expositions universelles*, by Geneviève Lacambre and Madeleine Rebérioux, Paris, Union centrale des Arts décoratifs, 1983.

■ *Le Musée d'Orsay*, Paris. Editions de la Réunion des Musées Nationaux, "Albums" collection, 1986.

■ *Les Pages du M'O*, series of 78 information cards in binder, Paris, Editions de la Réunion des Musées Nationaux (cards available to the public throughout the museum visit).
L'Opéra de Paris, Paris, Centre national de la photographie, 1985.

■ MANÉGLIER, Hervé: *Paris impérial, La vie quotidienne sous le Second Empire*, Paris, Armand Colin, 1990.

■ MATHIEU, Caroline: *Musée d'Orsay. Guide*, Paris, Editions de la Réunion des Musées Nationaux, 1986.

■ MONNERET, Sophie: *L'Impressionnisme et son époque. Dictionnaire international*, Paris, Robert Laffont, Bouquins collection, 1987, 2 vol.

■ *Musée d'Orsay; chefs-d'œuvre de l'Impressionnisme et du post-impressionnisme*, Paris, Editions de la Réunion des Musées Nationaux, 1984.

■ PASSERON, Roger: *Daumier, témoin de son temps*, Paris, Bibliothèque des Arts, 1979.

■ PINET, Hélène: *Rodin, Les mains du génie*, Paris, Gallimard, Découvertes collection, 1989.

■ REWALD, John: *Histoire de l'impressionnisme*, Paris, Albin Michel, 1986.

■ REWALD, John: *Le Post-impressionnisme*, Paris, Albin Michel, 1961, Paris, Hachette-Pluriel, 1987.

■ ROSENBLUM, Robert: *La Peinture au musée d'Orsay*, Paris, Nathan, 1989.

■ SESMET, Pierre: *1870-1871: "L'année terrible"*, Paris, Editions de la Réunion des Musées Nationaux, carnet Parcours No. 18, 1989.

Photographic credits:

Réunion des Musées Nationaux,
except for:
Fonds Urphot, p. 6-7, 10-11
Daniel Henry, p. 8-9
Sipa, p.38-39 (c) Moatti/Kleinesenn
Giraudon, p.97
Orsay Museum Press Department
(Jim Purcell), p. 10-13, 15, 20 & 26.

Printed in April 1994
by Snoeck, Ducaju and Zoon,
Ghent.
Text composed in *Walbaum*
by L'Union Linotypiste,
illustrations photo-engraved
by Bussière A.G. and paper made
by Papeteries Zanders
(Ikonorex mat 150 g).

Premier dépôt légal : janvier 1993
Dépôt légal : avril 1994
ISBN : 2-7118-2748-8
GM 20 2748